Sarah Webb

CHILDREN'S PARTIES

Illustrated by Terry Myler

THE CHILDREN'S PRESS

TO

Emily, John, Luan, Molly, Sean and Sam
– the next generation –
and to
Tanya, Andrew and Niamh

First published 1999 by
The Children's Press
an imprint of Anvil Books
45 Palmerston Road, Dublin 6

2 4 6 5 3 1

© Text: Sarah Webb 1999
© Illustrations: Terry Myler

ISBN 1 901737 18 7

Typeset by Computertype Limited
Printed by Colour Books Limited

Contents

1 Planning the Party

First step in successful party-giving is *planning*. And first step in planning is making a few essential decisions.

When?

Decide on a date. If it's a birthday party, the actual day is ideal or the nearest Saturday. Hallowe'en parties are most fun on Hallowe'en night.

Who and how many?

Decide who will be invited and list all the names. As the host only invite as many as *you* want to handle. Remember large parties are very tiring. Small ones with only special friends can be just as much fun. As children get older they may want to invite the whole class – be warned!

Where?

Decide on the venue. Your own house and/or garden is ideal. If you need more space you could ask a friend, or perhaps granny and granpa might help out. During the summer you may be able to hold your party in a nearby park, on the beach or in the woods. But always have an indoor venue available – just in case the weather doesn't co-operate!

7

Time?

Decide on a time. An early kick-off is ideal. By starting at 2.30 or 3 pm, your party should be over by 5 pm.

Length?

Decide on length. Younger children (under five) get tired easily so an hour and a half is about right; for older children about two hours.

Think of yourself too. *You* have to do all the entertaining, feeding, mummying and daddying and clearing up. After two hours *you* will certainly have had enough.

On page 14 there is a simple party 'plan' which splits the afternoon into the various activities.

Theme?

'Ordinary' parties demand less advance planning but can lack excitement. Theme parties are a great idea, especially for younger children. They love to dress up and simple costumes are easy to make. Whether it be a Cowboys' Ranch Party, Circus Fun, or a Rumble in the Jungle, the theme not only adds to the fun; it also helps to structure the party by fusing together all the elements, from invitations to food and games.

Chapters 4 to 6 describe different theme parties for different age groups. Or you could choose your own theme. A 'five' party for a five-year-old. A 'doggie' party for a dog enthusiast. You can use bits and pieces from the various chapters to put together a really original party.

Getting down to detail

Once you have made all the big decisions, you can plan the details. Remember that each theme party in the book has lots of brilliant suggestions under the various headings listed here.

Costumes

Every theme party suggests ideas for costumes. Make sure you also stock up on theme hats and masks in case a child comes out of costume and would like to join in the fun. Keep an eye on dressed-up children during the party. Spidermen and women, monsters or lions, can become over-heated in close-fitting costumes or plastic bin-liners.

Decorations

Keep them simple. Balloons and streamers are bright, effective and cheap. Just before the party, tie a couple of balloons on your gate or the nearest lamp-post to signpost your house. You'll find great ideas on decoration, from treasure maps to spooky spiders, in each theme-party chapter.

Food

Party food should be simple, tasty and fun (see the next chapter for easy party food and a useful guide to quantities). Remember that children's eyes are bigger than their mouths so portions should be kid-sized. For younger children (under five), make buns and cakes in small sweet-cases or in funny shapes such as animals or monsters. Sandwiches should be bite-sized. Older children (seven +) need more substantial food like chips, pizza and garlic bread, but don't forget sweet things too. Strangely coloured food is a big hit with all age groups; try green or purple icing on buns.

The ingredients to avoid are nuts, especially whole nuts, boiled sweets (small children can choke on these) and any strong or spicy flavourings.

The golden rule is to make as much as possible in advance and store in airtight containers or freeze. Keep food that has to be cooked on the day to the minimum – most foods to be served hot can be cooked in advance and kept warm in the oven.

Have plenty of cold drinks to hand – children get very thirsty racing around.

Going home presents

Need not cost the earth. A balloon decorated with a party theme (a skull and cross-bones, a cut-out star dusted with glitter), a packet of sweets, small masks or novelty items will be doubly exciting if presented in a bag that echoes the party's theme.

Helpers

Don't try to do everything yourself. For parties for very young children (under four) encourage the parents to stay and join in the fun. Teenagers, your child's favourite baby-sitter, a relative or neighbour, make very useful assistants and most will help for a modest sum – or nothing! Give them specific duties or jobs and get them involved in the games and fun – they will enjoy the party much more than if they are simply supervising.

Make one helper or parent the 'official photographer' to record all the special moments that you miss while mopping up orange on the floor.

Invitations

Making your own is much more fun than buying ready-made ones and gives you plenty of scope for 'theme party' originality. (There are lots of suggestions in chapters 4 to 7.)

Make sure they contain all the necessary information: date and day, time (both starting and finishing time), address, costume requirements (do stress that they should be simple), the name or names of the invited. And make sure parents, not just the children, get invitations. Include a simple map of how to reach your house – some of the parents may not know your local area.

Invitations should be sent out at least two weeks

To ....

You are invited to
Ann and John's
'Mad Hatter's Tea Party'
on Saturday 15th June
at 17 Castle Street, 2 to 4.30 p.m.
COME WEARING A MAD HAT!

PHONE 00 0000000

R.S.V.P.

in advance. RSVP at the bottom and your phone number will indicate that you want a reply. The phone number is also useful in case parents have any queries.

Music

Children love happy party music. Make tapes of your child's favourite songs or try your local bookshop for ready-made children's party tapes. Perhaps a musical friend could play the piano or guitar. Music is especially important for games like Musical Bumps and Pass the Parcel.

Prizes

Every game should have a prize or two. Stockpile these during the sales. Small toys, bubbles, novelty items and books are especially good.

Rest area

Set aside a special place for a resting, reading and quiet play area, with lots of cushions, books, toys, crayons and paper, A shy or quiet child may like to opt out of the games and a tired child may simply need a short rest.

Table settings

The table can be covered with a decorated paper tablecloth (see chapters 4 to 7 for ideas). If you haven't time to create one, pick up a party table-cloth at your local supermarket or shop. Paper plates (no washing up) and plenty of coloured napkins are essential. And keep lots of kitchen rolls handy for all those spills. Sturdy plastic beakers or mugs are less likely to be tipped over by enthusiastic reaching arms than paper cups.

Set a place at the table for each child, with a decorated place mat. Place cards are a good idea.

How much will it cost?

The main expenses are food, drink, decorations, prizes and going-home presents. If you want to hire a professional clown or puppeteer, they can be expensive but they certainly take the pressure off busy parents (see pages 137 to 140 for useful numbers and addresses).

One way of keeping cost to a minimum is to rope in enterprising friends and relations. You probably know someone who just loves baking party cakes and friends may, if asked, weigh in with crisps, soft drinks or small prizes.

To give an estimate of what your party should cost is almost impossible. How long is a piece of string? But a simple party for small children should not cost you more than £4 a head.

Make a party plan

It's essential to have a rough plan of the party on paper, even if you don't stick to it. List the games to be played, the prizes to be given, the time when tea will be served (so that sausages and hot food can be cooked or heated), after-tea activities. A simple plan might be:

3.00 Kids arrive. Present opening and general playing.

3.20 Games: Pass the Parcel, Pin the Tail on the Donkey, Blind Man's Buff, etc.

3.50 Party tea.

4.30 Less active games like Guess the Famous People, etc.

5.00 Going-home time, with presents.

5.30 Collapse on sofa!

Final countdown

Before the party

Do as much as you can before the actual day:

1 Make the costumes.

2 Buy or make the prizes and wrap them.

3 Make up the going-home bags.

4 Make name-badges and table decorations.

5 Prepare the games – wrap the parcel for Pass the Parcel, etc.

6 Shop for crisps and soft drinks and any other ingredients you need for cooking.

7 Make all food and store or freeze.

8 Clear the party area and remove all breakables.

9 Check you have the following on hand:

Kitchen roll for spills.

First-aid kit.

Spare pants and tracksuit bottoms in case of 'accidents'.

Black plastic sacks for rubbish.

Baby wipes for sticky hands and faces.

On the day:

1 Decorate the room if you haven't done this already.
2 Lay the party table.
3 Assemble the food and drink.
4 Hang balloons outside the gate.
5 Put a pencil and pad at the door, and as each guest arrives take the phone numbers of any parents who are leaving – just in case.
6 Have a final safety check on the party area:

No open fires.

No loose carpets or rugs.

No disinfectants or medicines within reach in the kitchen or bathroom.

Put away dogs or cats – noisy children are sure to frighten them.

Make sure there are no balls or toys on the stairs.

Close doors of rooms that are not in use – lock them if possible. Close any doors or gates to outside the house or garden.

Remove any keys from doors, especially the bathroom – children have a habit of locking themselves into the bathroom.

2 Easy Party Food

The following pages contain recipes for basic party food. All are easy to make and fun to look at and eat! They can be supplemented with shop-bought crisps, sausages, sweets and drinks.

Each theme party has its own special food ideas to add to the basic party food – look out for jungle juice and barm brac.

First, a rough guide to portions. Don't be surprised that ages two to six seem to eat more than ages seven to ten – younger children are usually accompanied by a mum and dad – and it's amazing how much *they* eat. So be prepared!

Remember – presentation is everything!

For each child aged two to six (with parent):

> 1 packet of crisps
> 4 cocktail sausages or 2 large sausages
> 4 small sandwiches
> 2 iced biscuits
> 2 top hats or chocolate marshmallows
> 2 chocolate krispie cakes
> 2 small buns or 1 large bun
> 1 helping of cake or ice-cream

For each child aged seven to ten:

  1 packet of crisps
  1 face pizza
  1 large handful of chips
  2 pieces garlic bread
  4 cocktail sausages
  2 top hats
  1 small bun or krispie cake
  1 portion of cake or ice-cream

Sandwiches Remove the crusts from the bread. Cut into small squares or try using shaped cutters – stars, animals and people.

Suggested fillings: grated cheese, sardines, tomato, tongue, meat paste, ham, chicken or turkey and egg mayonnaise (hard-boiled eggs mixed with mayonnaise).

Buns
(makes 24)

Small buns are easy to make and can be iced in different colours and decorated with sweets.

2 oz (50 g) soft margarine
2 oz (50 g) caster sugar
2 oz (50 g) self-raising flour
1 egg
Icing:
8 oz (225 g) icing sugar
about 2 tablespoons warm water
food colouring
sweets and cake decorations
bun cases

Preheat the oven to gas mark 4/ 180°C/350°F

Place all the ingredients in a large mixing bowl and beat together for 2 to 3 minutes. Place a tablespoon of the mixture in each paper bun case. Bake for 15 minutes and cool on a wire rack.

Place the icing sugar in a bowl and mix with warm water until a thick paste is formed. Colour the icing with a few drops of food colouring. Spoon on to the cool buns and add sweets or sprinkles.

You can make tiny buns by using paper sweet cases instead of bun cases.

Krispie cakes

Always a favourite! You can use cooking or plain chocolate but I prefer milk chocolate.

8 oz (225 g) milk chocolate
2 oz (50 g) Rice Krispies
raisins for decoration

Place the chocolate in the microwave until it melts, or melt in a ceramic bowl placed in a saucepan of boiling water. When the chocolate has melted add the Rice Krispies and stir gently until they are coated. Spoon into paper cases and leave to cool.

Fruit kebabs

Fruit makes a great snack and has the added bonus of being full of vitamins and minerals.

2 apples
2 oranges
1 melon
2 kiwi fruit
2 peaches
green grapes
juice of half a lemon

Prepare the fruit – peel and cut into bite-sized pieces. Put the fruit pieces on to wooden kebab sticks (available from the butcher's). Drizzle lemon juice over the apple pieces to prevent them from browning.

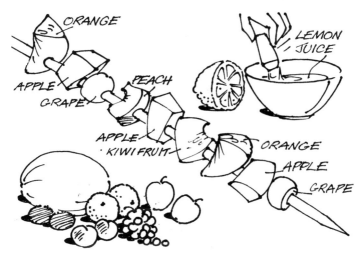

For a cool summer snack, place the fruit kebabs in the fridge for an hour before serving.

Basic sponge cake

The party cake is an important element in the party tea. More to look at, wonder at and enjoy than actually eat!

A basic plain or chocolate sponge forms a solid base and can then be decorated using icing, sweets, marshmallows, etc. (If you haven't time for baking, shop-bought sponges are more than adequate and can be cut into the required basic shape.)

The theme parties have their own special decorations but the basic recipe remains the same.

8 oz (250 g) soft butter or margarine
8 oz (250 g) caster sugar
4 eggs
8 oz (250 g) self-raising flour, sifted
1-2 tablespoons of milk

Preheat the oven to gas mark 4 /
350°F / 180°C

Grease a round 8 inch tin or two 8 inch sandwich tins.

Cream the butter and sugar together until light and fluffy. Beat the eggs in a small bowl and gradually add them to the mixture, beating well as you go along. Sift the flour into the mixture and carefully fold it in with a metal spoon. If the mixture does not easily fall from the spoon add a little milk.

Turn the mixture into the tin or tins and bake for 30 to 35 minutes if one tin is used, 25 to 30 minutes if two tins are used. To test if the sponge is ready press the centre of the cake gently; if it springs back it's cooked.

Remove from the oven and cool on a wire rack. Decorate with icing, made by mixing icing sugar with warm water.

To make a chocolate cake, add 1 tablespoon of sifted cocoa to the flour.

If your sponges don't rise properly, add a level teaspoon of sifted baking powder to the flour.

Number cakes	Use your ingenuity to create cakes that give the birthday age.

Cut sponge cakes or Swiss rolls or bake sponge cakes in different tins to create the pieces. For example: for a '7' use two long loaf tins (halve one to form the short side); for an '8' use two cakes baked in ring tins or cut large holes in two round sponge cakes.

Ice with coloured butter or glacé icing. Decorate with Smarties, Jelly Tots, and cake decorations.

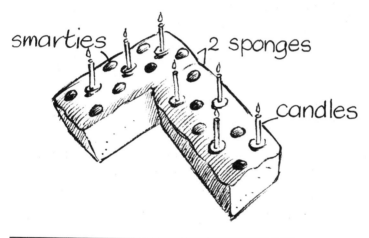

Potato mashers, potato boats	2 large potatoes 8 oz (250 g) grated red cheddar 4 oz (125 g) butter 4 tablespoons of milk salt and pepper

Cover large potatoes in tin foil and cook in the oven, gas mark 6 / 200°C / 400°F, for 1 to $1^{1}/_{2}$ hours until baked. Cut in half lengthways and scoop out the insides. Place in a large bowl and add the cheese, butter, milk, salt and pepper and mash together. Sweet corn, pieces of ham or bacon give extra flavour. Spoon the mixture back into the potato skins.

To make the 'boats', add a small paper sail threaded on to a cocktail stick.

Caterpillar cake

4 chocolate Swiss rolls
1 packet of chocolate finger biscuits
1 packet of Smarties
a small amount of icing sugar

Cut the Swiss rolls in half and place each piece on a long plate, flat side down. Curve the 'caterpillar' in the middle. Give each segment a pair of chocolate finger 'legs'. At the front give him chocolate finger 'feelers' and add Smartie eyes stuck on with a little glacé icing (icing sugar mixed with a little warm water). Add candles.

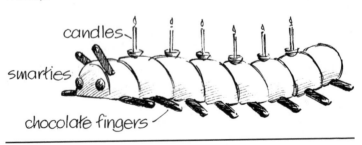

candles
smarties
chocolate fingers

Ice-cream

Ice-cream is always a top party favourite. Shop bought ice-cream can be decorated with sweets, cones and wafers or chocolate sauce. Or you could try making your own yummy strawberry ice-cream.

1 tin strawberries
6 oz (175 g) caster sugar
1 teaspoon lemon juice
1/2 pint (275 ml) cream
fresh strawberries (optional)

Open the tin of strawberries and pour out one third of the juice. Place the remaining juice and the strawberries in an electric blender with the sugar and lemon juice. Swoosh together for 1-2 minutes until creamy.

Pour the cream into a mixing bowl and whip until peaks begin to form on the surface.

Pour the strawberry mixture into the cream and blend together with a metal spoon. (Add a handful of fresh halved strawberries at this stage.)

Pour the mixture into a shallow metal dish and place in the freezer until set (2-3 hours depending on the freezer).

Remove the ice-cream from the freezer 10-15 minutes before serving.

The amazing train

An easy but impressive looking cake for younger children.

2 shop-bought chocolate Swiss rolls
Chocolate butter icing:
8 oz (225 g) soft butter
16 oz (450 g) icing sugar
2 level teaspoons cocoa powder
1 packet of chocolate mini-rolls (6)
1 box of Smarties
1 packet of Rolos
1 packet of Maltesers
birthday cake candles and holders

Blend the cocoa powder with 2 tablespoons of boiling water and allow to cool. Beat the butter with half the icing sugar until smooth. Beat in the rest of the icing sugar with the cocoa powder mix and a tablespoon of milk if necessary.

Spread the icing over one of the Swiss rolls to make the 'engine'. Place it gently on to two of the chocolate mini-rolls – the 'wheels'.

Cut one third off the second Swiss roll and cover it with icing. Place it at one end of the 'engine', sticking it in place with lots of icing, to create the 'train driver's cabin'. Add a chocolate mini-roll 'funnel' to the other end. Add Smarties to decorate and two Rolo 'buffers' at either end.

To make the 'coal truck', scoop out a hole in the second piece of Swiss Roll and cover the whole with icing. Place it on two chocolate mini-roll 'wheels'. Fill the hole with Malteser 'coal', sticking the sweets together with icing to create a heaped pile. Add Smarties and Rolo 'buffers'. Place the candles on the top of the 'train driver's cabin'.

You could also make a chocolate finger biscuit 'railway track'!

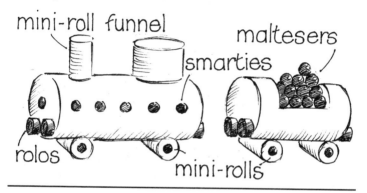

mini-roll funnel
maltesers
smarties
rolos
mini-rolls

Hot bread

This delicious bread is easy to make and makes a tasty snack for kids and parents too.

1 French stick
4 oz (125 g) butter
pinch of salt
$\frac{1}{2}$ teaspoon of pepper
1 tablespoon mixed herbs
1 teaspoon lemon juice
2 cloves crushed garlic (optional)

Preheat the oven to gas mark 6 / 200°C / 400°F

Cut the bread into slices an inch thick. Mix the butter, herbs, salt, pepper, lemon juice and crushed garlic and spread over both sides of the bread. Press the pieces together to reform the stick, wrap in tin foil and bake for 15-20 minutes and serve hot.

Sausages   Cocktail sausages are delicious and fun. Prick each sausage and cook in the grill or oven until brown and crispy.

Sausage rolls To make sausage rolls, wrap uncooked sausages in puff pastry. If you are using frozen pastry allow it to thaw out at room temperature. Cook sausage rolls for 30 minutes in a preheated oven (gas mark 6 / 400°F / 200°C).

Chocolate biscuit cake

A delicious chocolate cake that requires no baking.

8 oz (225 g) digestive biscuits
1 oz (25 g) raisins, cherries and chocolate chips
4 oz (125g) milk chocolate
4 oz (125 g) butter
2 tablespoons double cream

Line a shallow cake tin (8 inches) with tin foil. Press carefully around the edges and be careful not to break the foil.

Put the biscuits in a large mixing bowl and break them into small pieces. Add raisins, cherries and chocolate chips (1 oz of each ingredient).

Place the chocolate in a saucepan and heat gently. Add the butter and the cream and stir on a low heat until all the ingredients have melted together.

Pour the mixture over the biscuits and stir gently. Pour into the cake tin and cover with foil. Leave in the fridge for 2 hours until set.

Home-made popcorn

Buy a packet of popping corn (available in most supermarkets) and cook according to directions. Add a sprinkle of salt and serve warm. Delicious!

Biscuits
(makes 10)

Cut the dough into shapes to suit your party – stars for a Space Party, animals for a Jungle Party.

1 oz (25 g) caster sugar
3 oz (75 g) plain flour, sifted
2 oz (50 g) soft butter or margarine
Icing:
2 oz (50 g) icing sugar
1-2 tablespoons of warm water
food colouring
sweets and cake decorations

Preheat the oven to gas mark 4 / 180°C / 350°F

Place the butter and sugar in a mixing bowl and beat together until light and creamy. Add the flour and mix well. Place the mixture on a floured surface and knead until smooth. Roll the mixture out thinly and cut into shapes. Place on a floured baking tray and bake for 10–15 minutes until golden brown. Cool on a wire rack.

Mix the icing sugar with warm water and mix to a thick paste. Add a few drops of food colouring. Spoon on to the biscuits and decorate.

Top hats

1 packet of chocolate
1 packet of marshmallows
1 packet of Smarties

Melt the chocolate in a bowl in the microwave or over gently boiling water. Put a teaspoon in each paper sweet case, filling it half way up. Add a marshmallow and finish with a drop of chocolate and a sweet.

Face pizzas   Easy pizzas for cheats!

Buy small ready-to-cook pizzas and add toppings to make funny faces – extra cheese, pepperoni, pineapple, salami, mushrooms, tomatoes and peppers.

3 Party Games

Choose games to suit the number of children and the age-group. For young children (two to four), keep the games simple with easy rules. Vary the pace, with noisy jumping-and-dancing games followed by quieter sitting-and-thinking games.

With older children, different games can be introduced, although don't forget the familiar favourites. Each theme party has its own games like Bobbing Apples for Hallowe'en and Pass the Teddy at the Teddy Bear's Picnic.

Toddlers to Fours

Balloon in the Air – 3+
Give each child a blown-up balloon. The aim of the game is to keep it in the air without letting it touch the ground. The winner is the child who manages this for the longest time.

Farm Animals – 3+
You need – a farmyard story with lots of animals in it – make one up and write it out or try a children's storybook.

Each child becomes a farm animal and must remember their special noise – cows go 'moo', ducks go 'quack' and so on. The adult storyteller reads the story and the children join in with their own noise. At the end of the story let all the animals join in together and make lots of noise! It is a good idea to have a 'practice' run before the real game to make sure all the children understand.

Find the Pair – 3+

You need – large bright recognisable pictures from magazines (pictures of toys, animals, trees and so on), thin card, paper glue and scissors.

Stick the cut-out pictures on to the card and cut each into two pieces or 'pairs'.

Hide one half of each pair around the room or garden. Give the other half of the pair to each child. The first child to find the other half of his or her pair wins. Small children may need some help with this game – you could give the younger children an older 'partner' to assist them.

Heads and Shoulders, Knees and Toes – 2+

A fun action song. While singing the children must touch the part of the body that is mentioned. Each verse gets faster and faster until everyone gets confused! Here are the words:

Heads and shoulders, knees and toes,
Heads and shoulders, knees and toes,
    Knees and toes,
And eyes and ears and mouths and nose,
Heads and shoulders, knees and toes,
    Knees and toes!

The Hokey Cokey – 2+

Children of all ages enjoy the Hokey Cokey!

Everyone joins hands, adults and children alike, in a large circle. Drop hands and follow the actions in the song. During the chorus, join hands and swing your arms up and into the middle of the circle and down and out again. Here are the words:

You put your left leg in,
    You put your left leg out,
In, out, in, out, and shake it all about.
    You do the hokey cokey and you turn around,
    And that's what it's all about – oy!

Chorus –
    Oh, hokey cokey cokey!
        Oh, hokey cokey cokey!
    Oh, hokey cokey cokey!
        Knees bend, arms stretch, ra ra ra!

Follow with –
    You put your right leg in ...
    Chorus
    You put your left arm in ...
    Chorus
    You put your right arm in ...
    Chorus

And finish with –
    You put your whole self in,
        You put your whole self out,
    In, out, in, out, and shake it all about.
        You do the hokey cokey and you turn around,
        And that's what it's all about – oy!

Hunt the Sweets – 2+

This is a treasure hunt for tiny tots. Simply hide the sweets – small wrapped soft sweets and chocolates – around the room or garden area. Make sure there are plenty of hidden 'treasures', at least two for each child. Send the children around the room to find the easy-to-discover sweets.

Mad Dancing – 2+

A game with no set rules. The children dance and there are prizes for – the best dancer, the funniest dancer, the most graceful dancer and so on. This is a great game for burning off excess toddler energy!

Musical Bumps – 2+

Clear an area of the room or, if possible, play outside. Choose a suitable piece of lively party music and ask the children to dance, skip and jump about. When the music stops they must sit down. The last to sit down is 'out'.

It's a good idea to encourage the 'out' children to continue dancing – perhaps a special dancing prize could be awarded – otherwise they may feel left out.

Musical Islands – 3+

Another relation of Musical Bumps. Place 'islands' – cushions or sheets of newspaper – on the ground, one for each child. The children dance around the islands and when the music stops they each sit on one. Every time they begin dancing again, remove an island. The child who can't find an island is 'out'. The winner is the child who gets the last island.

Musical Statues – 3+

Musical Bumps for an older age-group. Instead of sitting down, the children must freeze like statues when the music stops.

Pass the Parcel – 2+

You need (for two games) – newspaper or old wrapping paper, sellotape, two main prizes, and a handful of small prizes – wrapped sweets, small toys, etc.

Wrap the main prizes in paper. Keep wrapping the parcel, adding a small prize every few sheets, until the parcel is big.

Sit the children in a circle on the floor. When the music stops the child with the parcel can unwrap a layer of paper. Try to ensure that each child has at least one turn at unwrapping!

Pin the Tail on the Donkey – 3+

You need – a large sheet of stiff paper or card, a thick black marker, a 'tail' made of paper or string, blue-tack.

Draw a large donkey on the card. (For a theme party change the donkey and tail to a teddy bear and bow-tie or a lion and tail and so on.)

Make a tail and place a large piece of blue tack on the end.

Each child is blindfolded in turn and must try to pin the tail on the donkey's rump. Mark each attempt with the child's initials. The child with his or her initials nearest the correct place wins.

Ring a Ring o' Roses – 2+

Another fun singing game. Children and adults stand in a circle holding hands as they sing. They all fall down when 'down' is sung and jump up when 'up' is sung. Here are the words:

Ring a ring o' roses,
   A pocket full of posies,
Atishoo, atishoo,
   We all fall down.

Picking up the daisies,
   Picking up the daisies,
Atishoo, atishoo,
   We all jump up.

What's the Time, Mr Wolf – 3+

Mr Wolf stands back to the children, who start at their 'home' (a large sofa or a clear piece of wall). They creep towards him, saying, 'What's the time, Mr Wolf?' at intervals. Each time he turns and responds 'It's 3 o'clock' or 'It's 5 o'clock'. But if he says 'It's dinner time,' he runs towards them and tries to catch as many as possible before they reach home. The winner is the last child to be caught.

Fives to Sevens

Balloon Battle – 5+

You need – a 'net' (string) and a balloon.

Divide the children into two teams. Place a piece of string across the room to act as a net. The aim of the game is to keep the balloon in the air, passing it backwards and forwards between the two teams. If the balloon drops to the floor or bursts on one side, the other team wins a point. The winner is the team with the most points after ten minutes.

Balloon Race – 6+

You need – deflated balloons, string.

Divide the children into two teams. Place the deflated balloons and a piece of string for each child at one end of the room or garden.

Each team member runs in turn to the balloons, blows one up, ties it to a piece of string, then runs back 'home'. The first team with all its members home, each with a balloon, wins the game.

Blind-Man's-Buff – 6+

Pick one of the children to be the blind man and cover his or her eyes with a soft scarf. The other children must dodge the outstretched hands and avoid being caught. When the blind man catches a child he or she must guess who it is. If the guess is correct the captured child becomes the next blind man. (This game needs a clear space.)

The Conga – 6+

This is a great way to burn off excess energy and have some fun. Play some lively party music (Latin American if possible). The adult leader leads the conga snake of children around the house or garden, each holding the leading child's waist or shoulders. The leader takes a few steps, then side kicks with the left leg. A few more steps, then a side kick with the right leg, and so on. The 'snake' weaves around obstacles, dancing and kicking.

Dead Ants – 6+

A version of Musical Bumps for older children. The children dance around the room and when the music stops they become dead ants – lying on the floor with their arms and legs in the air. The last child to become a dead ant is 'out'.

The Doctor's Dog – 7+

A fun memory game, using adjectives instead of nouns. This time each child adds an adjective to describe the doctor's dog, using a new letter from the alphabet, from A to Z. For example: 'The doctor's dog is an adorable dog ... a beautiful dog ... a cool dog...' and so on.

Egg and Spoon Race – 6+

You need – tea-spoons and hard-boiled eggs or potatoes.

This game is best played outdoors or in an empty hall or corridor. Place the eggs on the spoons and give one to each child. The children race to the marked finish and the first one home wins.

Funny Folk – 6+

You need – A4 sheets of white paper, coloured pencils or markers.

Give each child a sheet of paper and some pencils or markers. Ask him or her to draw a head and neck on the paper and not to show it to anyone. It can be human, animal, or alien, the funnier the better. The paper is then folded over once to hide that drawing and passed to the next child. He or she draws a body from the shoulders to the top of the legs, folds it and passes it on. Finally the legs and feet are added and passed on.

When the pictures are opened, everyone can look and laugh at the 'Funny Folk' they have drawn.

Grandmother's Footsteps, One, Two, Three – 5+

Grandmother (an adult or older child) stands facing the wall with her back to the children. The children stand at the opposite wall and begin to creep up to her. When grandmother turns they must freeze on the spot. Anyone who moves has to return to the starting wall. The first child to tap grandmother on the back wins.

Hide and Seek – 5+

This popular game can be played indoors or outdoors. One child becomes the 'seeker' and counts to one hundred while the other children run away and hide. The seeker shouts 'coming', then looks for the hidden children. The last child to be found is the winner. Some children hide so well that they have to be called out of hiding as no one can find them!

I Drove To Dingle – 6+

A simple memory game for youngsters. The children sit in a circle and begin each turn with 'I drove to Dingle to see Fungi and I packed ...' Each child must add an item to the suitcase, taking a new letter from the alphabet, from A right down to X, Y and Z. For example ... apple, ball, cat, dog, emu, fishing-rod and so on. For older children, try asking them to remember all the previous suitcase contents before adding their own – not an easy task!

Mexican Piñata or Bash the Bag – 5+

In Mexico at Christmas time colourful animal-shaped 'piñata' are made from clay. These decorations are hollow and are filled with sweets and coins. At the end of Christmas children smash open the piñatas with sticks, showering everyone with goodies.

You need – a strong paper carrier bag, small prizes such as sweets, chocolate coins and toys, newspaper, a wooden spoon and string.

Place the prizes in the bag and fill with scrunched up newspaper. Hang the bag securely from a door post or tree.

Give each child two or three turns to hit the bag with the wooden spoon. Eventually the bag will split and the prizes will spill out for the lucky child. You could decorate the bag with coloured markers.

The Quiet Game – 5+

This is a good choice to calm down over-excited children.

Ask the children to sit on the floor with their eyes closed. Ask each child a question in turn, such as 'Sally, do you like sweets?' or 'Sam, is your hair pink?' The child must remain quiet and still, without giggling or answering the question. The quietest and stillest child wins.

Sardines – 6+

A similar game to Hide and Seek. One child hides while the others count to one hundred together and then separately begin to look for him or her. When they find the hidden child they squeeze in – like sardines. The game continues until all the children are hiding with the original child. The winner is the first child to find the hidden person. Then he or she becomes the 'hider' in the next game.

Simon Says – 5+

An adult or older child becomes Simon. He gives orders, each time starting with the phrase 'Simon says.' For example: 'Simon says touch your head,' or 'Simon says turn around.' But when an order is issued without the 'Simon says', like 'Touch your toes,' any child who responds is 'out'.

Three-legged Race – 5+

You need – scarves and/or neckties.

This game is best played outdoors as a lot of space is needed. Pair off the children and tie their inside legs together with a scarf or necktie. Encourage each pair to practise walking and running together, then race them to a marked finish. First home wins.

Eights to Tens

Alphabet Race – 8+

You need – pencils or pens and paper.

Give every child a piece of paper and a pen. The guests must write down as many items as possible in a given category with the given letter, for example animals beginning with A, or girls' names beginning with B. Have several rounds, using different letters and categories. The winner is the child with the most items on his or her list. This game could also be played in teams of three or four.

Charades – 9+

Split the guests into two teams. One member of a team is given the title of a film or book by the adult 'judge' and must act out that title for their team mates in a given length of time. Titles should be reasonably simple – three or four words at most. The team with the most correct guesses wins.

These are signs which the teams can use:

Book – place the hands together, palms facing up.

Film – place two fists together and wind one like a film projector.

Number of words in the title – hold up the correct number of fingers.

'The' – make the shape of a 'T' with two fingers.

Small words such as 'a', 'and', 'or', 'of' – indicate small by almost pinching the thumb and forefinger together.

Name – pat the head with your hand.

'Sounds like' – pull your ear.

'I'll be acting out the whole title' – make a big sweeping circle with the arms.

Consequences – 9+

You need – long sheets of paper, pens or pencils.

Give each child a piece of paper or pencil on which is written a sequence such as:

There was a boy called ...

Who met a girl called ...

At ...

He said ...

She said ...

They went to ...

And the consequence was ...

The first child writes in the boy's name, then folds the paper over and passes it on to the next child who fills in the girl's name, and so on to the end.

When the sheets are finished each child reads out the story in turn, often with hilarious results.

Another sequence could be:

The film is called ...
It was written by ...
The stars were ...
Male lead ...
Female lead ...
The story was about ...
The music was ...
The acting was ...
And the film was ...

Draw the Word – 8+

You need – large sheets of paper, a thick black marker.

Divide the children into two teams. One team must think of a word, the harder the better, such as curtain, lizard, rose or oak-tree. One member from the other team is told the word and must draw it for their team mates, who have two minutes to guess it. Each team takes turns drawing and guessing. The team with the most correct guesses wins.

Famous Pairs – 9+

You need – pictures of famous and well-known 'pairs' or things that belong together, such as chickens and eggs, Barbie and Ken, Zig and Zag, dogs and puppies. Stick each half of the pair on a separate piece of thick paper or card.

Give each child three or four halves of a pair and

hide the others around the garden or room. The first child to join all their pairs correctly wins.

Feely Game – 8+
You need – a large cardboard box with a hole cut in the side, objects such as an orange, a comb, an egg-timer, a fork, a rubber glove and so on.

Ask each child in turn, with eyes closed, to place his or her hand in the hole and to close their eyes. Then put three of the chosen objects in the box. The child must identify the objects by the texture and shape (set a time limit for this). The other children will have fun hearing the guesses and seeing if they are right or wrong. Try some difficult objects such as a light bulb or a kiwi fruit. The child who correctly names the most objects wins.

At Hallowe'en try using slimy or cold, wet objects such as cold spaghetti, a packet of frozen peas or a chicken fillet for a really spooky Feely Game.

Guess What – 8+
You need – a pre-recorded tape of interesting sounds

– taps dripping, paper tearing, a dog, a cat, a baby crying, a bottle opening, pieces of well-known music or songs and the voices of famous actors or politicians; sheets of paper and pencil or pens.

Give each child a pencil or pen and a sheet of paper. Ask the children to identify the sounds they hear. Play the tape, pausing for a little while between each sound-bite. The winner is the child with the most correct sounds.

Guess Who – 8+

You need – two large sheets of paper, pictures and photographs of famous/well-known people from the world of television, cinema, music and politics, pictures of parents and teachers themselves when babies; sheets of paper and pencil or pens.

Stick each picture or photo on a large piece of paper. Number each and hang the paper on the wall. Give each child a pencil or pen and a sheet of paper. Ask them to identify each picture in a given length of time and write the answers on their sheet. The child with the most correct answers wins. This game could also be played in teams of three or four.

Like the Word – 9+

Split the children into two teams. One team decides on an adverb – for example: slowly, quickly or gently. The second team issues orders to jump, run, eat and so on 'like the word'; they must then try to guess the adverb from the other team's actions. The teams then swap over. The team which correctly guesses the most adverbs wins.

Limbo Dancing – 9+

You need – a broom handle or a piece of bamboo.

Supple youngsters make very good limbo dancers. Play some fun music, Caribbean if possible, in the background.

Ask two adults or older children to hold the stick or broom handle. The children line up and take turns to limbo under the stick. Anyone who touches the floor with their hands or who touches the stick is out. The winner is the dancer who goes the lowest. Encourage the adults to join in and add to the fun.

Mad Footie – 8+

You need – big wellies or big shoes (a pair for each child), a small ball, such as a tennis ball, and two 'goal-posts'.

Divide the children into two teams. Each child must put on a pair of old wellies or shoes. The idea is to try and score a goal with the tiny ball, through a small goal marked with goal-posts. This game is best played outside. If playing inside, try it with huge fluffy slippers and a balloon.

Mummies – 8+

You need – lots of old wrapping paper and news-paper, two rolls of sellotape.

Divide the guests into two teams. The aim of the game is to cover one team member in paper from head to toe, leaving the face uncovered, like a 'mummy'. The first team to totally cover their chosen victim wins.

Outdoor Scavenger Hunt – 8+

You need – a list of objects (such as a small stone, a daisy, a feather, a round leaf and so on, depending on the garden), and a plastic or large paper bag for each pair or team.

Divide the children into pairs or teams. Give each a list of items to collect and a plastic or paper bag. The children must find as many of the listed items as they can within a given time. The team or pair with the most items wins.

Remember, Remember – 8+

You need – a tray with a number of objects on it – an apple, a shoe, a toy animal, a pencil, a ring, a shell, and so on – a pencil or pen and paper for each child.

Give each child a pencil or pen and a piece of paper. Bring in the tray with the objects on it and place it in the middle of the room for one minute.

Ask the children to remember all the objects, then remove the tray. Give them three minutes to write down all the objects they remember. The winner is the person with the most correct objects on his or her list.

Sack Race – 8+
You need – cloth sacks.

Race the children from one end of the room or garden to the other. Run heats if the space or the sacks are limited. The children can hop, run, wiggle or jump to the finishing line.

Smelly Game – 8+
You need – saucers, strong-smelling food (garlic, coffee-beans, polo mints, washing powder, chopped banana, chopped onion, perfumed soap), pens and paper.

In a separate room to the party guests, place each 'smell' on a saucer and put the saucers in a row on the table. Blindfold each child and lead them to the table. Ask them to sniff each saucer and tell them to remember each smell. Outside the room, remove the blindfold and ask them to write down all the smells that they can remember. The child with the most correctly identified 'smells' wins.

Suitcase Dash – 8+
You need – two suitcases, each filled with a hat, a top, a skirt or trousers, a pair of boots or shoes, a jacket or coat and a pair of sunglasses – all large sizes and the sillier the better.

Split the children into two teams. Place the suitcases at one end of the room or garden. Each child must run up to the suitcase, put on every piece of clothing, shoes and sunglasses, take them off, put them back in the suitcase and run back to his or her team. Then it is the turn of the next child and so on. The winners are the first team with all their team mates home.

This is a game which all kids love – make sure to have the camera or video camera ready to catch the madness.

Treasure Hunt – 8+

You need – clues on pieces of thick paper or card, treasure (a bag of gold chocolate coins).

Place the clues around the party area. Try and place them in different rooms or areas of the garden to prevent the children from following one another. Make them suitable for the particular age-group. Some can be straightforward – 'look in the top drawer'; anagrams – 'look under the elbat' (table); or crossword-type clues – 'look under what lights your way' (lamp). The clues should follow each other in a logical manner and should not be moved or taken away.

Divide the children into pairs or teams and give each a copy of the first clue. The first team to complete the hunt finds – and keeps – the treasure.

4 Toddlers to Fours Parties

Teddy Bear's Picnic

Today's the day the teddy bears have their picnic, either outdoors in fine weather or indoors. Each child can bring his or her own special teddy to join in the party games and food.

Invitations

You need: thin yellow card, large coloured envelopes, scissors or a craft knife and a black marker.

ribbon

- Trace out teddy pattern on card.

- Cut out carefully and use as a template to make more cards.

- Add eyes and a mouth and write the party details on the back.

Costumes

Paint each child's face as a teddy bear. Some children do not like paint on their faces so paint a tiny teddy or teddy face on their hands instead.

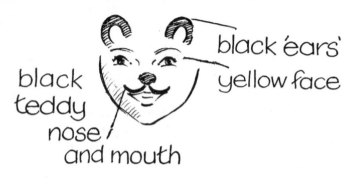

black 'ears'

yellow face

black teddy nose

and mouth

Decorations, Music and Name-badges

Place bright rugs or tablecloths on the floor, or if outside on the ground, to sit on.

Balloons and streamers look great inside and out, on trees and picnic tables or on the walls and door posts. Cut out teddy shapes and hang them from the ceiling and walls (out of reach of over-enthusiastic hands!).

Teddy bear 'music' could include songs from *Winnie the Pooh*, the *Teddy Bear's Picnic* song and the *Goldilocks and the Three Bears* story on tape (produced by Ladybird and available at bookshops).

Give each child a teddy bear name-badge cut from yellow card.

front

Joe

sellotape

back

safety pin

Games

Add these special teddy party games to other favourites.

Musical Teddy Bears: Musical Bumps with a difference. The children dance, skip and jump around. When the music stops the child and his or her teddy must sit down together. The last child to sit down is 'out'. It is a good idea to encourage all the children to continue dancing even if they are out – perhaps you could award a special dancing prize.

Hunt the Teddy: Hide all the teddies around the party area. Ask the children to find their own teddy and the first pair (teddy and child) to be reunited wins.

Teddy Dancing: Each child dances with his or her teddy. Prizes are awarded for the best child dancer, the best teddy dancer, the funniest child dancer and so on.

Teddy Bear's Picnic Food

Spread the party food on brightly coloured rugs or tablecloths. (If the children are very young, a table is safer and less messy.) If possible place a small tray on each rug to put drinks on to avoid spills. Cut out teddy place-name cards on yellow card for each child – a teddy head or a teddy body. Keep the

menu simple – the special teddy foods and two or three other treats such as crisps and popcorn, Rice Krispie cakes and top hats. Place small portions of each food in a dish on each rug and refill when necessary.

Teddy biscuits: Cut biscuit dough into teddy shapes using a cutter or a sharp knife. When baked, decorate with currants for eyes, nose and mouth.

Teddy buns: Cover the tops of plain buns with glacé icing (icing sugar and water) with a few drops of yellow food colouring added. Add Smarties for eyes, liquorice strands for the mouth and glacé orange slices for ears.

Teddy sandwiches: Make honey, chocolate spread and marmalade sandwiches – just what Pooh Bear and Paddington Bear would ask for.

A delicious teddy cake: Cover a large round sponge cake with butter icing. To give a deeper yellow colour add a few drops of yellow food colouring.

For the butter icing beat together 4 oz (125 g) butter with 8 oz (225 g) icing sugar, added little by little. If needed, add 2 tablespoons of milk.

biscuit ears

liquorice strand mouth

sweets

Decorate teddy's face with large liquorice sweets for eyes and nose, black liquorice strands for a mouth, and piles of digestive biscuits stuck together and covered with butter icing to make the ears.

Going-home Presents

A small brown paper bag with handles can be decorated with a simple ribbon and filled with teddy treats. Try tiny teddy jellies, teddy bear chocolates, a small teddy bear book or notebook (Pooh Bear, Rupert the Bear and Paddington are all popular choices.)

Now it's picnic time for teddy bears!

Rumble in the Jungle

There's a rumble in the jungle. The lions, tigers, snakes and elephants are all coming out to play. Jungle parties are great for younger children. They can dress up as their favourite animal and play lots of fun jungle games.

Invitations

Lion invitations are easy!

You need – yellow card, a craft knife or scissors, a black felt pen and large coloured envelopes.

- Draw a lion shape on to card (see page 57) and cut it out.

- Use this as a template to make more invitations.

- Draw a lion's face on one side of the card and write the party details on the other.

- You could add a yellow wool 'mane'.

You can make elephants from grey card, snakes from green card and tigers from orange card with black stripes drawn on in black felt pen.

Costumes

Animal costumes are simple to put together. First choose your animal:

Lion: Dress the child in yellow and add a 'mane' made of yellow wool attached to a thin strip of material. Add a lion's face, by painting with face paints. (See page 115.)

'mane' around head

strip

wool strands

Elephant: Dress the child in a grey tracksuit or grey tights and jumper. Attach large grey material or paper ears to a hair-band to make 'ears'. For a trunk, tie together three loo-paper tubes and paint them grey. A piece of elastic will hold the 'trunk' in place.

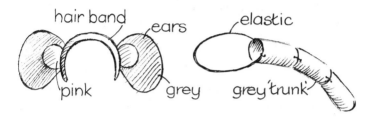

Snake: Dress the child in green. Paint the face green with face paints – metallic if possible. You could even spray the hair green. Add a long pink painted-on tongue and a pair of plastic fangs (Dracula fangs from a joke shop).

Decorations, Music and Name-badges

Decorate the party area with large green leaves cut out of paper or card. Add huge 'flowers' made of coloured tissue paper. 'Vines' can be from green net and strips of material.

Party music could include the soundtrack from Disney's *The Jungle Book* and lots of animal songs such as 'Nelly the Elephant'. Real animal sound tapes are also available or try recording your own from nature programmes for an authentic jungle feel!

Give each child an animal-face badge made from thin card. Sellotape a safety pin on to the back.

Games

Sleeping Lions: Ask the children to become 'sleeping lions' by lying flat on their backs, completely still. Choose two to become 'wakers'. They must creep around the lions and try to make them move or laugh, without touching them. They can pull funny faces, tell jokes and act silly – anything goes. The last two lions to respond win and then become the next 'wakers'.

Tortoise Race: You need – a pillow or large cushion for each child.

Give each child a pillow. If there are more children than pillows, run heats. Line them up on their hands and knees and place a pillow on each of their backs. They must race along a given course, around the room or garden. If they drop the pillow they must start again. The first tortoise home wins.

Feed the Lion: You need – a large paper carrier bag, string, a black felt tip pen, old newspaper.

Draw a lion's face on the paper bag and tie it to the back of a heavy chair. You could add a yellow wool 'mane' to your lion. Make small balls from the newspaper. Each child throws three or four balls into the mouth of the hungry lion (the opening of the paper bag). The winner is the child who scores the most 'baskets' into the mouth.

Jungle Food and Cake

Decorate the table with a large green paper tablecloth. Add large 'flower' place mats cut from coloured paper or card. Give each child a jungle 'leaf' place card.

Place plastic toy animals on the table – snakes, lions, tigers and elephants. Drape green paper or material 'vines' from the ceiling or from a central lamp.

Cucumber crocodile: Cut teeth into one end of a cucumber. Slice a piece off the bottom to help it sit. Add two big olive or pickle eyes. Push cooked cocktail sausages on sticks into your cucumber to create crocodile scales.

Animal sandwiches: Cut cheese, ham, egg and other filled sandwiches into animal shapes using shaped cutters.

Animal biscuits: Cut the biscuit dough into animal shapes before baking (see biscuit recipe on page 30).

Ice in different colours and decorate with sweets and silver balls for eyes.

Jungle fruit kebabs: Make tasty and healthy kebabs from fruit threaded on to wooden skewers (see page 20 for recipe).

Jungle punch: Make a refreshing 'jungle juice' from a mixture of orange and apple juice with added fruit chunks – apple, orange, pineapple and grapes.

Lion cake: Cover a plain round sponge with yellow butter icing (see page 26). Add a 'mane' made from sweet wafers cut or broken into triangles. Add eyes – sweets on biscuits – and half biscuit ears. Black liquorice strands cut to size make realistic whiskers.

Going-home Presents

Decorate small paper bags with green jungle leaves and coloured flowers cut from paper. Fill with sweet jelly snakes, a tiny toy animal, seeds to grow their own 'jungle' (mustard and cress seeds) and animal bubble-bath or soap.

Let those lions roar!

5 Fives to Sevens Parties

Circus Fun

Roll up, roll up, all the fun of the circus – clowns, lions, tigers, elephants and the Big Top combine to provide a fun-filled party.

Invitations

For clown faces you need – white card, markers, large envelopes, scissors, wool, paper glue.

- Cut circles out of the card to make the faces.

- Draw clown features on the front and write the party details on the back.

- Add wool hair (see page 58).

Costumes

Circus costumes can be easily created with a little imagination. Clowns are a popular choice but your child could also dress up as an acrobat, strong man or ring-master.

Clown: Dress the child in a stripy top, with coloured or stripy tights. Add a pair of old, big and baggy shorts or cut-up trousers. Add braces, a silly hat and oversized shoes. Paint his or her face white and add a red nose and mouth. Or you could invent your own original clown face. Here are two – there's another on page 2.

Acrobat: Dress your girl in a leotard, tights and ballet shoes. Add a ruff of net or a bright silky scarf tied in a bow around the acrobat's waist. Decorate her face with glitter, pink lipstick and pink cheeks.

Strong man: Dress the boy in a black leotard or black vest and leggings. Add a tunic of fake fur or one cut out of brown paper with painted-on black leopard spots. Make fake 'dumb-bells' from two large black circles and some bamboo.

fake fur
tunic

Ring-master: Dress the child in black or dark trousers, white shirt, bow-tie and a bright waistcoat. Complete the outfit with a top hat decorated with silver tin-foil stars and a tailed dinner jacket. Add a whip or a riding-crop, or create your own with a piece of bamboo with string attached.

Decorations, Music and Name-badges

Decorate the party area with bright balloons and streamers. Cut out circus animals – elephants, lions and tigers – from coloured card and hang on walls and from door posts. Make clown faces on paper plates, using markers, wool and gummed shapes. Draw clown faces on balloons and hang from the ceiling. Hang streamers from a central lamp to simulate the ceiling of the Big Top.

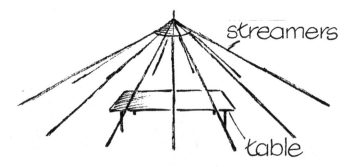

Play jaunty 'circus' music. It may be possible to buy circus or carnival music from large music stores or you could use nursery-rhyme tapes or other fun children's tapes. Animal tapes such as 'Nelly the Elephant', or the *Lion King* songs are also appropriate.

Make clown face name-badges from card. Decorate with wool hair.

Circus Games

In addition to the other party games, try these special ones with a circus fun-fair theme.

Feed the Clown: You need – bean bags, small balls,

a large cardboard box, markers, scissors.

Take a large cardboard box and on one side draw a clown's face with a large, gaping mouth. If the box has printing on it, staple or stick on brightly coloured paper.

Cut out the clown's mouth. You could add wool hair, gummed shapes, tin-foil stars and other decorations to the clown's face and the box.

Place the child behind a given line. Each throws three balls or bean bags at the box, trying to put them through the clown's mouth. The child who throws the most balls into the mouth wins.

Coconut Tin Shy: You need – a clear, empty space with no breakables, such as a corridor or hall or the garden, a collection of empty tins or drink cans, bean bags or small balls.

Place the tins or cans in a stack to form a pyramid shape. Each child throws a bean bag or ball at the pyramid. The winner is the child who knocks over the most cans.

Hoopla: You need – stiff card, several tall bottles.

Make hoops with stiff card cut into strips and

secured with sellotape. Place tall bottles in a pattern. Each child throws three rings from behind a given line and tries to hoop the bottles. The winner is the child who hoops the most bottles.

Lucky Ducks: You need – bamboo, a large metal hook, washing-up bowl and plastic ducks which can be bought cheaply in most 'pound' or toy shops.

This game requires some preparation but it's worth it. Make a 'fishing rod' with a piece of bamboo with a large metal hook added. Mark the underside of one duck with an X. Place the plastic ducks in a washing-up bowl half filled with water.

Each child takes a turn to hook a duck, which is more difficult than it sounds. The winner is the child who hooks the lucky duck.

Juggling Peas: You need – plastic or paper cups, plastic drinking straws, dried peas.

Give each child a small plastic or paper cup and a drinking straw. Place a large pile of dried peas in the centre of the room. Each child sucks up as many peas as possible and drops them into his or her cup, within a given length of time. The winner is the child with the most peas. A good team game .

Circus Food and Cake

Decorate the table with a brightly coloured paper cloth. Give each child a top hat place mat cut from black paper or thin card. Hang streamers over the table, write each child's name on an inflated balloon and attach it to their chair.

Popcorn cups: Make up the popcorn according to the instructions on the packet. Lightly salt and place in large paper cups. Use brightly coloured cups or decorate plain ones with stars, stripes, clown faces and circus animals.

Clown face biscuits: You need – large digestive biscuits, icing sugar, silver balls, sweets and other cake decorations.

Ice each biscuit with glacé icing (icing sugar mixed with water). Decorate each to resemble a clown's face – the faces on pages 56 and 62 will give you some ideas.

Clown ice-cream: You need – vanilla ice-cream, sweets (Jelly Tots and Smarties), ice-cream cones, cream in a can.

Place a scoop of ice-cream on a plate or in a dish. Place a cone 'hat' on top and add eyes and a mouth with the sweets. Squirt cream around the clown's head to create a fun ruffle.

ribbons

Big Top cake: You need – round sponge cake, icing sugar, a knitting needle, thin coloured ribbons in different colours

Ice the cake with glacé icing. You could add a few drops of food colouring in your child's favourite colour. Place the cake on a flat plate and put a knitting needle in the centre. Attach thin coloured ribbons to the needle and secure them under the cake plate. Add ribbons all around the cake to give the illusion of a circus tent.

Top hats: See recipe on page 30.

Going-home Presents

Decorate a small paper bag with silver stars or add a brightly coloured bow. Circus presents could include – balloons, bubble mixture, a yo-yo, tiny 'magic' tricks, joke books and red clown noses.

Mad Hatter's Tea Party

In *Alice in Wonderland* by Lewis Carroll, the Mad Hatter, the March Hare and the Dormouse have a tea party. Alice joins them in the fun, and answers riddles and strange questions. A Mad Hatter's Tea Party is easy to organise and children love wearing silly hats. And yes, the parents and helpers must wear them too!

Invitations

You need – coloured card, in 2 or more contrasting colours, scissors, black pen, paper glue and large envelopes.

- Cut out top hats and hat-bands from the card, using the diagram as a guide.

- Glue a contrasting coloured band on each hat and write 'Come to the Mad Hatter's Tea Party' on the hat-band.

- Write the party details on the back of the hat – and don't forget to ask the party guests to wear a silly hat.

Costumes

Basic costume requirement is a mad hat. You could adapt a plain hat in many different ways. Add coloured paper, card or material spots or blotches in a random or fixed pattern; add coloured wool pom poms; add huge tissue paper flowers. Another idea is to spray an old bowler hat or felt hat gold or silver, and add glitter.

silly hats

Decorations, Music and Name-badges

There are many *Alice in Wonderland* characters and motifs which can be used to decorate the party in style. Huge poster-sized playing-cards can be hung on the walls and stuck on doors – with added heads if you have a budding artist in the family! The original John Tenniel *Alice in Wonderland* drawings,

or other Alice pictures, could be photocopied, enlarged and used to decorate the party area in an original way. Cut mad hats from card, in lots of different shapes and sizes. Decorate with glitter, sticky shapes and paint and thread on to string or elastic. Hang from the ceiling or doors.

The Disney *Alice in Wonderland* soundtrack would make ideal background music (try a larger music store or tape from the video). You could also play a collection of 'Nonsense' rhymes, including those by Lewis Carroll. There is an excellent 'Nonsense' collection on tape in the Ladybird range.

Cut small top hat name-badges from coloured card and write the names around the base to create a hat-band. Add a safety pin with sellotape. Or you could fasten a piece of coloured card with the child's name on it to his or her hat or tuck it into the hat-band if there is one.

Games

Pass the Hat: Seat the children in a large circle on the floor and play party music. When it stops the child left holding the hat is 'out'. The last child 'in', wins.

Make-a-Hat Game: Divide the children into teams of three or four. Give each team newspaper, old magazines, coloured paper, old wrapping paper, empty toilet rolls, sellotape and scissors. Ask each team to design and model a mad hat. The maddest creation wins.

Musical Hats: Place assorted hats on the floor and play party music. When it stops the children must put on a hat. Any child who is hatless is 'out'. Remove one or two hats each round. The last child 'in' wins.

Party Food and Cake

Hat sandwiches: Cut assorted square sandwiches into the shape of top hats, by trimming the sides.

Top hats: See recipe on page 30.

March hare and dormouse biscuits: Use rabbbit and mouse cutters to shape the biscuit dough before baking. Ice the biscuits in bright colours using glacé icing (see page 19) and add silver balls for eyes.

Top hat cake: Cut a large round sponge cake to resemble a top hat. Ice with dark brown chocolate butter icing (see page 26). Make a wide hat-band using Smarties and Jelly Tots.

Going-home Presents

Fill a small paper bag, tied with a brightly coloured ribbon, with a miniature pack of playing cards, a chocolate mouse or rabbit, a plastic pocket watch and a couple of chocolate and marshmallow top hats.

Hopefully none of the guests will quote Alice: 'It's the stupidest tea party I ever was at in all my life!'

Space Fun

'There's life, Jim but not as we know it ...'

Aliens, space ships, stars and planets – space parties are great fun and can spark the imagination of any child. Get in lots of silver foil and paint and prepare for action.

Invitations

For star or planet invitations you need – thin yellow card, large coloured envelopes, scissors, glitter, paper glue and a black marker or pen.

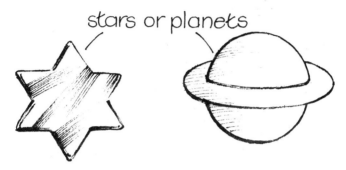

stars or planets

- Cut star or planet shapes out of the yellow card.

- Write the party details on one side of the shape.

- Dot the other side with glue and sprinkle with glitter.

Costumes

Spacemen: Spacemen (or women) need a helmet and a space suit. A grey or plain dark tracksuit is ideal. Add wellies (you could spray old ones with silver paint) and a silver belt (cover an old one with tin foil or spray silver).

To make a helmet – spray a cardboard box silver and cut out a rectangular 'visor'. Add star shapes and space symbols. Or borrow a motorbike helmet and add tin-foil stars.

Aliens: Aliens come in all shapes and sizes. Put

together a costume in a chosen colour – green, purple or blue – with tights, tee-shirts and track-suits. Make 'space-boppers' from a plastic head-band, tin wire and ping-pong balls. Paint the alien's face and hands in your chosen colour and add strange alien features to their face. (See page 117).

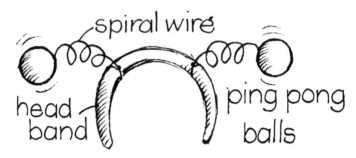

Decorations, Music and Name-badges

Cut large stars and planets out of thin, coloured card and decorate with glitter. Hang from the ceiling and over the party table. Large paper lampshades can be bought and decorated as planets with silver spray and glitter. Spray balloons silver or add silver glitter to black balloons, and hang from the ceiling. Make a 'lunar landscape' by covering the floor with old, crumpled sheets. Place small soft toys or balls of newspaper under the sheets to create lumps and bumps. You could even give your landscape its very own black holes – pieces of black plastic or card – or lunar lakes of tin foil.

Atmospheric music such as New Age relaxation tapes is ideal. Or compile your own space tape with music from *Star Trek* or *Star Wars* and 'space' songs like *Girl From Mars* by Ash. Mums and Dads, and their friends, could have hours of fun thinking of song ideas for a space tape.

Each child could invent his or her own space name, to be written on a star-shaped card badge. For example: Simon Spock, Space-age Sally, Violet from Venus, Lunar Larry.

Games

Musical Stars: Cut large 'stars' from tough white paper and spray silver. You could use tin foil but it tends to rip after one game. This game is played like musical chairs but when the music stops the children must sit on a star. Remove one star after each musical interval. The child on the last star when the music stops wins.

Space Memory Game: Place 'space' items on a tray. You could use a star, a tiny space figure, a silver lunar rock, a ping-pong ball ('the moon') and a water pistol ('space gun'). This is played like the normal memory game. (See page 50.)

Space Walking: You need – 2 inflated balloons for each child, string.

Tie a balloon to both ankles of each child. The children must walk around the room, trying to burst each other's 'alien' balloons. The winner is the last child with his or her balloons intact.

Some children are afraid of bursting balloons; place them in the 'space' corner – a rest area filled with books, toys, paper and pencils.

Pass the Space Parcel: Wrap the present in layers of silver foil and coloured paper. You could add a sprinkle of star dust (glitter) to some of the layers. When the music stops the child who is holding the parcel unwraps a layer.

Space Food and Cake

Decorate the table with a paper tablecloth sprayed silver; place star and planet shapes on the cloth before spraying and lift off after to give a two-tone effect. Give each child a silver metallic dish to put their treats in. Make place cards from star-shaped coloured card.

Stick your child's name on the ceiling with luminous stars and watch the faces when you dim the lights! Hang 'stars' and 'planets' – cut-outs and balloons – over the table.

Snackeroos: Milky Way bars and mini Mars bars, Monster Munch and other 'alien' space snacks.

Biscuits and sandwiches: Use a star-shaped cutter to create space-shaped food.

Martian fizz: Add a scoop of ice-cream to Coke or 7-Up and watch it fizz.

Easy lunar landscape cake: Take a large round sponge cake and cover it with white butter icing (see page 26). Create peaks, lumps and bumps to give a craggy 'lunar' effect. Place a collection of Lego space figures with their space buggy on the cake. You could also add one or two hidden 'alien' figures. Add a small flag made from a cocktail stick and paper.

A perfectly yummy cake for all space enthusiasts.

Going-home Presents

Make a 'space pack' in a small bag or box. Decorate it with stuck-on stars. Give each child a Milky Way or Mars bar, UFO sweets, a Lego spaceman, luminous star stickers for their bedroom, and/or a small book on space.

6 Eights to Tens Parties

Treasure Island Pirates

Sixteen men on a dead man's ship,
Yo ho ho and a bottle of rum.

Sail the seven seas with your own gang of rufty-tufty cut-throats. Pirate parties are very popular and create lots of great opportunities for treasure hunts, pirate food and adventure games.

Invitations

You need – black card, white paper, black marker, paper glue, large envelopes, scissors.

scull and cross-bones

- Cut the black paper into folded invitations.

- Cut out a skull and cross-bones for each card from the white paper.

- Stick the skull and cross-bones on to the front of the card.

- When dry, draw in gaping holes for eyes, a black nose and jagged teeth, with the black marker.

- Write the party details inside the invitations.

Costumes

Basic pirate: A stripy tee-shirt or top, old ripped jeans, boots (black wellingtons or riding boots are ideal). Add a red bandanna on the head or around the neck, and gold hoop earrings. For pirate eye-patches, cut a circle out of black paper or card; attach elastic to the patch and adjust to fit.

A pirate cutlass can be made from card covered with silver foil. Paint black stubble on to the face and make elaborate moustaches with face paint, black eyeliner or a mascara wand.

Decorations, Music and Name-badges

Cut large palm-tree leaves out of green paper and attach to doors and walls. Cut out big skull and cross-bones motifs from white paper and stick on sheets of black. Cut triangular shark fins out of black paper or card and place them on the floor. Make a skull and cross-bones for the front door. Draw smaller ones on balloons to hang outside and around the house.

Play the *Treasure Island* audio book in the background. For younger children try the *Muppet Treasure Island*. Old ballads and rousing folk songs will also set the scene.

Give each child a pirate's flag name-badge, adding a pirate name: Jolly Roger, Cut-throat Ciara, Scary Sam and Black-eyed Zoe!

Games

I Went on a Pirate Raid: A fun alphabet game. The children sit in a circle and begin each turn with the prefix 'I went on a pirate raid and I took a...' Each child must add an item to the sentence, taking a letter from the alphabet, from A right down to X, Y and Z. For example: axe, bottle of rum, cutlass, dagger and so on. Awards can be made for the funniest or the most original addition.

Treasure Island: Adapt Treasure Hunt (page 52) and give it a pirate slant with jewels as well as gold coins for treasure. The clues could use words such as 'deadman', 'chest', 'rum', 'cutlass'.

X Marks The Spot: You need – a large sheet of paper, markers, coloured magazines, scissors, paper glue.

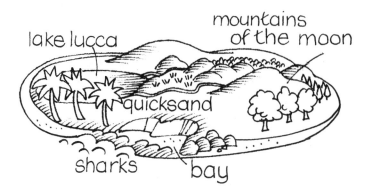

Draw a 'pirate map' on a large sheet of paper, with lots of hills, mountains, lakes, rivers, rocky areas, trees, bays, cliffs, swamps, jungles and quicksand (your child may like to help prepare the map). You could add cut-out buildings, trees, fish and animals from colour magazines such as *National Geographic* or travel brochures. On the back of the map mark an X where the treasure is buried, making sure that it can't be seen from the front.

Each child in turn guesses where the treasure is buried and marks the spot with a cross and his or her initials. The child whose cross is closest to the treasure wins.

Flags on the Beach: You need – sand (or earth), pebbles and plants for decorations, cocktail sticks, paper, markers, scissors, paper glue, sheet of paper.

Another fun 'find the treasure' game'. Place damp sand in a shallow tray, a large box, a seedling tray or even a metal baking tray. Make a 'map' of the sand on a piece of paper and make a mark where the treasure is buried. Decorate the sand with small pebbles and stones, leaves and flowers (jungle plants), a small container of water (a lake) and plastic jungle animals. Make flags by sticking triangles and squares of paper to cocktail sticks.

Each child places an initialled flag in the sand where he or she thinks the treasure is buried. The winner is the child whose flag is the closest to the treasure, as marked on the map.

Pirate Food and Cakes

Cover the table with a white tablecloth on which you have drawn a 'Treasure Map' with markers and magazine cut-outs. Fill the sea with fish and sharks' fins. Decorate each paper plate with a skull and cross-bones. Place a shoe box covered with foil in the centre of the table and fill with treasure – old jewellery, gold chocolate coins and wrapped sweets.

Pirate biscuits: Decorate large digestive biscuits with white glacé icing (see page 19). Add Smartie eyes, black liquorice moustaches, polo mint earrings and hundreds and thousands 'stubble'.

Pirate boats: Cut small rolls in half and spread with peanut butter or chocolate spread.

Pirate galleons: You need – cucumber, celery sticks, can of tuna, cream cheese with chives, mayonnaise, grated cheese, tin of chopped pineapple, a sheet of white paper, markers, scissors, paper glue and cocktail sticks.

Cut small triangles and squares from white paper to make 'sails' and 'flags'. Draw skull and cross-bones designs on the sails and flags on the squares. Thread or stick the paper on to the sticks.

Cut the celery sticks and cucumber into two-inch bits to make 'boats'. Scoop out some of the insides of the cucumber and cut a small slice off the bottom of the 'boats' to prevent them from falling over.

Mix together the tuna, mayonnaise, grated cheese and pineapple and spoon into each boat. Place a sail or flag in every boat and serve.

Pirate cake: Ice a round sponge cake. Decorate the top to look like a pirate's face – large eyes made of sweets, a black card eye-patch, hundreds and thousands 'stubble' and a head bandanna of red card.

Pirate galleon cake: You need – an 8 inch round chocolate sponge cake (see page 22), chocolate butter icing, Smarties or round liquorice sweets, Maltesers, white paper, 3 knitting needles, candles and candle holders.

Make the butter icing by mixing 2 level table-spoons of cocoa powder and 1 tablespoon of milk into a paste. Cream 4oz (100g) soft butter with the paste and gradually add 10oz (275g) of icing sugar. Beat the mixture until it is smooth and creamy, adding a little more milk if necessary.

Cut the chocolate sponge cake in half and sandwich the two halves with some of the chocolate butter icing. Slice a small piece off the rounded end so that the 'ship' will stand up. Cover the cake with the rest of the chocolate butter icing and run a knife along the sides to create a wooden plank effect.

Make portholes with round liquorice sweets or Smarties and use the candles as 'guns' shooting from the sides of the ship. Thread squares of white paper on to knitting needles as sails and top one with a skull and cross-bones flag. Stick the sails into the top of the cake. Arrange the cannonballs (Maltesers) in a heaped pile on the deck and stick together with butter icing.

Going-home Presents

Fill a small brown 'booty' bag with presents and tie the top with a piece of string or a ribbon. Treasure could include – gold chocolate coins, toy jewellery, fake moustaches, eye-patches and necklaces and bracelets of sweets.

Cowboys' Ranch Party

In modern times cowboys use trucks, jeeps and even helicopters to round up the herd. But they are still renowned as skilled horsemen, horse-breakers and 'whisperers'. Cowboy parties combine all the legend and romance of the Wild West with a tasty 'ranch' barbecue and lively 'cowboy' games.

An outdoor setting with lots of space and a barbecue area would be ideal.

Invitations

For cowboy hats you need – thin brown or yellow card, brown or black wool, paper glue, scissors and large envelopes.

- Cut cowboy hat shapes from the card.

- Glue wool around the hat to make a hat-band.

- Write the party details on the back of the hat.

Costumes

Cowboy costumes can easily be put together from everyday clothes and accessories. Start off with denim jeans, a checked or denim shirt and a plain coloured leather or suede waistcoat. Add a cowboy hat, a bright red bandanna and boots, leather if possible, or black wellies.

The cowboy could have dark stubble – use face paint or an eyeliner pencil. He or she could carry a lasso rope or come complete with a horse (a borrowed hobby horse). For a sheriff, add a badge, leather gloves and a gun.

Decorations, Music and Name-badges

A cowboy party is best held outdoors. Decorate the area with balloons and streamers. To give an authentic Western feel, make 'Wanted' posters and attach them to walls and trees. You could use a photo of the birthday child as the wanted outlaw!

For an indoor party, decorate with plastic cowboys and Indians, as well as balloons, streamers and 'Wanted' posters.

Country and Western music is classic cowboy music – from Johnny Cash to Garth Brooks. You could even organise your own line dancing.

Give each child a Western name-badge, cut from yellow card in the shape of a sheriff's badge – Sheriff Joe, Bad Bill, Wild Jane and Four Gun Sophie.

Games

Horseshoes: This traditional cowboy's game is still played in the American outback. If you can't get your hands on any horseshoes, try using heavy wire rings instead.

You need – 2 metal stakes and 4 horseshoes.

Divide the children into two teams. Place the stakes in the ground and line the first team up four or five feet away from them. Each team member throws the horseshoes at the stake in turn. The other team then take its turn. The team with the most 'hits' at the end wins.

Make sure there are no children playing near the stakes.

Cowboys and Indians: You need – rope or thick string.

Divide the children into two teams – cowboys and Indians. The cowboys tie all the Indians except one, the 'Chief', to trees, each other or garden furniture. The Chief must untie all his Indians and he is timed. The Indians then tie up all the cowboys except their 'Sheriff', who has to untie them. The quickest rescuer wins.

Children love tying each other up – but check that the rope is not hurting anyone.

Cowboy Hide and Seek: This is played like the normal Hide and Seek, except this is a case of the Sheriff finding the outlaws. As each outlaw is found he or she goes to 'jail', a designated area of the garden or house. The last to be found wins.

Food

Food is an important part of a cowboy party. Decorate the table, outdoor or indoor, with a bright, checked tablecloth and red and yellow-coloured paper napkins. Place the food in baskets or metal containers. Decorate the table with plastic cowboys and Indians.

This food is especially suitable for a barbecue but can also be cooked indoors.

Beans and sausages: Cook sausages over the barbecue and serve with baked beans in metal containers.

Barbecued potatoes: You need – 1 large potato for each child.

Cut each child's initial into the skin of a large potato. Brush each potato with oil and sprinkle with salt. Wrap in two layer of foil and cook in the charcoal for 40-45 minutes, turning occasionally.

Serve with butter, grated cheese and mayonnaise.

Toasted marshmallows: You need – 2 packets of marshmallows.

Toast each marshmallow over the barbecue on a long skewer. Turn frequently until they are lightly golden. Serve with ice-cream.

Sausage wagon wheels: You need – 8 slices of brown bread, 6 oz (150 g) cream cheese, 2 tablespoons of tomato ketchup, 8 cooked sausages or 16 cooked cocktail sausages, salt and pepper.

Cut the crusts off the bread carefully. Place the ketchup, cream cheese and a pinch of salt and pepper in a mixing bowl and beat together. Roll out the bread using a rolling pin and, when flat, spread with the cream cheese mixture.

Place a sausage (or 2 cocktail sausages) at one end and roll the bread around it carefully. Press down the final end of the bread firmly. Wrap each roll in tin foil and chill in the fridge for one hour. Cut the rolls into one inch 'wagon wheels' and serve.

Sweetcorn ranch salad: You need – 2×11 oz (326g) tins of sweetcorn, 4 large tomatoes, 4 spring onions, 4 tablespoons of mayonnaise and salt and pepper.

Cut the tomatoes and spring onions finely. Drain the sweetcorn. Mix all the ingredients in a large bowl and season to taste.

You could also serve – hamburgers in buns, spare ribs or chicken drumsticks, all cooked on the barbecue.

Make sure everything is thoroughly cooked.

Going-home Presents

Tie the presents up in thick brown paper, with string. Include – sweet cigarettes, a sheriff's badge and handcuffs, toy cowboys and Indians, a book of cowboy stories or a book about horses.

Go get 'em, Cowboy!

7 Parties for all Ages

A Christmas Party

Christmas is one of the best times of the year to have a party for children. Decorations – trees, lights, wrapped presents, holly and ivy – may already be in place. Father Christmas or 'Santa' can visit the party and there are many tasty Christmas party recipes and fun party games to choose from.

Ding dong merrily on high,
In heaven the bells are ringing.

Invitations

For Jolly Snowman invitations you need – thin white card, black paper, red paper, scissors, paper glue, cotton wool, black marker and large envelopes.

- Cut snowmen out of the white card, making sure that they fit into your envelopes.

- Cut circles out of the black paper to make eyes, buttons and noses.

- Cut hats, mouths and boots out of the red paper.

- Write the invitation details on the card.

- Cover the other side with glue and blob pieces of cotton wool all over until covered with 'snow'.

- Stick on the eyes, mouths, noses, hats, buttons and boots on to the snowman.

You could also make 'holly' cards using green card with red paper berries, or 'Christmas tree' cards using green card with a yellow star and baubles.

Costumes

For a Christmas party paint the children's faces with seasonal themes (see page 116). You could also try red-nosed Rudolphs or snowmen.

black nose   white

white
card

antlers

red
nose

brown

hair
band

Decorations

Most of us decorate our houses for Christmas. For a party, push out the boat with some extra-special ideas.

Silver stars: you need – old card (cereal boxes are ideal), paper glue, scissors, tin foil, string.

Cut star shapes out of the card. Cover with tin foil and stick down the edges if necessary. Pierce a hole at the top of a point and add string to hang up your star.

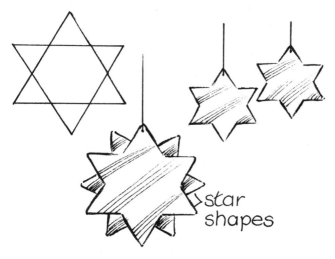

star
shapes

Silver bells: You need –
scissors, paper glue, old
cardboard egg cartons,
tin foil, string.

Separate the egg carton
into segments. Cover each
'bell' with silver foil. Pierce
a hole in the top and add
string to hang up your 'bell'.   silver foil

You could also spray pine-cones with gold and silver paint and make snowflakes from white paper squares folded and cut.

Christmas lanterns: You need – red, white and green rectangles of thick paper or thin card, scissors, sellotape, paper glue, silver and gold glitter, a newspaper.

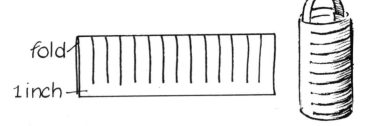

fold

1 inch

For each lantern take a rectangle of paper or card, roughly 10 inches by 5 inches. Fold the rectangle in half lengthways and cut lines into the folded side, leaving an inch to the end. Open the rectangles and glue the ends to each other.

Cut a small strip of the same coloured paper to make a handle. Sellotape each end into the top of your lantern. Put blobs of glue on your lantern and sprinkle glitter over it (put newspaper under to catch the excess glitter). Hang the lanterns across a room, in doorways or on the walls.

Christmas crackers: You need – red paper or red crepe paper, old cardboard toilet-roll tubes, wool, scissors, paper glue, glitter, sellotape, tiny presents and sweets.

Place the toilet rolls on the red paper. Leave 4 inches at either end. Roll the paper around the tube and secure with sellotape. Twist the paper at one end and secure with a piece of wool.

Pop the present and sweets into the cracker, twist the paper and secure the end. You could also add a joke written on a small piece of paper. Snip the paper at both ends. Put some glue on the centre of the cracker and sprinkle with glitter (put something under the cracker to catch the excess).

Gummed shapes or shapes cut out from coloured paper will give your cracker a professional finish.

Music

Christmas songs and carols are available on tape and CD. You could also have a Christmas sing-song. Children of all ages enjoy singing *Rudolph the Red-Nosed Reindeer*, *Jingle Bells*, *Away in a Manger*, and *When Santa Got Stuck up the Chimney*. And you could help them with *The Twelve Days of Christmas*. Here are the words:

On the first day of Christmas
My true love sent to me
A partridge in a pear tree.

On the second day of Christmas
My true love sent to me
Two turtle doves and a partridge in a pear tree.

On the third day of Christmas
My true love sent to me
Three French hens, ...

On the fourth day of Christmas
My true love sent to me
Four calling birds, three ...

On the fifth day of Christmas
My true love sent to me
Five gold rings, four ...

On the sixth day of Christmas
My true love sent to me
Six geese a-laying, five ...

On the seventh day of Christmas
    My true love sent to me
    Seven swans a-swimming, six …

On the eighth day of Christmas
    My true love sent to me
    Eight maids a-milking, seven …

On the ninth day of Christmas
    My true love sent to me
    Nine ladies dancing, eight …

On the tenth day of Christmas
    My true love sent to me
    Ten lords a-leaping, nine …

On the eleventh day of Christmas
    My true love sent to me
    Eleven pipers piping, ten …

On the twelfth day of Christmas
    My true love sent to me
    Twelve drummers drumming, eleven …

Games

Fan the Snowflake (age 5+): You need – old newspapers, scissors and thin white paper.

Cut the snowflakes out of small squares of paper. Fold a square into quarters and make triangular nicks in the paper – now you have snowflakes. Give each child a folded newspaper and a snowflake. The children must fan the snowflakes along the ground, using the newspaper. The winner is the first snowflake to the finishing line.

Flying Angels (3+): This is played like Musical Statues, except that when the music stops the children must become 'flying angels', with their arms lifted to shoulder height. The children who move their 'wings' are out.

Christmas Pairs (6+): You need – card, scissors, paper glue, Christmas pictures that belong in pairs.

Make the pairs by gluing two matching couples or things that belong together on to a piece of card. Use Christmas theme pictures: Baby Jesus and the stable, holly and red berries, a candle and a flame and so on. Cut the pairs in half and hide one half around the room.

Give each child one half of the pair, and ask them to find the other half. The first child who does is the winner.

Father Christmas (all ages!): An adult could dress up as Father Christmas and visit the children. Costumes can be hired or put together, using old clothes and a little imagination!

Christmas Food

Cover the table with a bright paper tablecloth. Cut squares and rectangles out of Christmas wrapping paper and stick on to the tablecloth. Silver foil stars would be very dramatic on red. Christmas plates can be bought or you could decorate paper plates with a green card Christmas tree or a silver foil star. Add bright bows of scrap paper or ribbon to the top of each present.

Children's place cards can be made in the shape of a Christmas tree.

Christmas tree sandwiches: Make up sandwiches with the chosen filling. Cut into Christmas trees using a special cutter.

Snowmen biscuits: Cut the dough into snowmen shapes before baking, using a small and larger circular cutter. Ice, when cool, with white icing and add silver balls to make eyes, nose, mouth and buttons.

Also serve traditional Christmas food, such as mince pies, Christmas cake and plum pudding.

Going-home Presents

Make small Christmas stockings from two pieces of thin red card glued together. Fill with sweets, chocolates and a tiny, wrapped Christmas present – a toy, book or game.

Hallowe'en

Hey ho, it's Hallowe'en,
Ghosts and witches to be seen,
Demons, banshees, red and green,
Hey ho, it's Hallowe'en.

At Hallowe'en (31 October) children of all ages enjoy dressing up and playing spooky games. So it's a great time to have a party.

For a long time people believed that on this night witches, ghosts and spirits roamed the earth for the night. It was originally known as 'Festival of the Dead'. The church tried to make it into a Holy Day rather than a heathen festival and renamed it 'All Hallow's Eve', which later became Hallowe'en. Huge bonfires were lit to scare the terrors away and to burn the witches flying past on their broomsticks!

In ancient Ireland the Druid leaders gathered at a place called Tlachtga, near the Hill of Tara. They built a huge Holy fire and every fire in Ireland was supposed to be put out and relit using fire from the Druidic blaze. Only then could Ireland be safe from evil.

Hallowe'en was also a time for magic and fortune-telling. Many young men and women tried to discover who they would marry by eating a piece of barm brac with charms added – a ring meant an impending wedding.

So enter into the spirit of the night. Dress up and act up. It's Hallowe'en!

Invitations

For pumpkin heads you
need – orange card, black
paper or card, paper glue,
scissors, black felt pen,
large envelopes.

- Cut the orange card into
  'pumpkin' circles.

- Cut triangular eyes, noses and mouths out of the
  black card.

- Stick the faces on to the pumpkins and write the
  party details on the back.

Other ideas: a witch's hat, a black cat or a 'cauldron'.
Write the party details in gold or silver pen.

Costumes

Witches, wizards, monsters, ghosts, Dracula – there's
no shortage of Hallowe'en characters, and you can
buy marvellous masks.

Witch: A black top and flowing black, dark red or
purple skirt, black tights and boots, lace-ups if
possible. Add a flowing cape and a witch's hat and
broomstick. To give added spooky scare, dangle
plastic spiders and bugs from the hat-brim.

Wizard: Black top and black, dark purple or green
trousers. Add a flowing cape and a wand. For extra
effect, add star and moon shapes cut from yellow
material or silver paper to the cape.

A Flowing Cape

1. Take a large square of
   fabric and fold in ½ twice

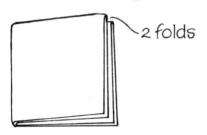

2 folds

2. cut a small curve here

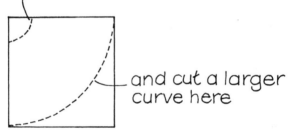

and cut a larger
curve here

3. Open out the cape and cut
   open to the neck. Hem
   the edges and add a draw string
   to the neck.

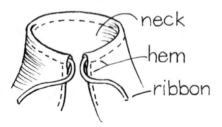

neck

hem

ribbon

A Witch's Hat

1.

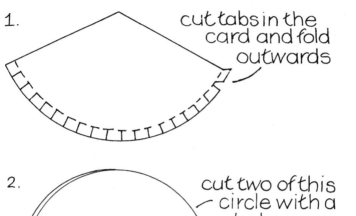

cut tabs in the card and fold outwards

2.

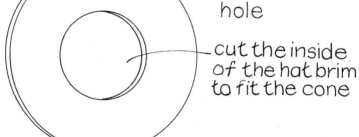

cut two of this circle with a hole

cut the inside of the hat brim to fit the cone

3.

roll the cone up and stick the sides together

stick the tabs to each of the hat brims

You could give your witch or wizard a green or light purple face with face paint. Spooky!

Monster: Scary monsters can be created from all kinds of clothes and accessories. Dress the children in one strong colour – purple, red or green – and paint their faces the same colour, using face paints. Attach paper spots and blotches made from paper or material or paint matching coloured spots on their faces. Add plastic fangs, nails and a material or card tail.

Ghost: A ghost costume can be easily made from an old sheet, with eye holes cut out. Make sure the sheet is not too long for smaller children or else they may trip while walking.

Dracula: Dress an older child in an old dinner suit, complete with white shirt and bow-tie. Paint the face white, using face paint or talcum powder, and slick back the hair with hair gel. Add white plastic fangs and paint blood dripping from the corners of the mouth. Gruesome!

Decorations

Hallowe'en decorations must above all be spooky! Cut out witches and cats from black paper. Hang them from the ceiling and stick them on the windows.

Dim the lights and create an eerie atmosphere with night-lights in jam jars placed around the room. Replace lamp bulbs with green, blue or red bulbs. Make 'scary' spiders with your child and hang them from the ceiling. Carve a pumpkin head and place it in your front window.

Scary spiders: To make 6 spiders you need – 1 cardboard egg carton, paper glue, black paint, paint brush, 24 pipe cleaners, thin elastic, 12 small white buttons.

- Cut the egg box into the 6 segments and trim around the base of each to create a spider's body.

- Paint each spider and all the pipe cleaners with black paint and leave to dry.

- Cut each pipe cleaner in half.

- Using a sharp pencil or a pen, poke four small holes in each side of the spider and add pipe-cleaner 'legs'. Secure each leg by bending the pipe cleaner against the inside of the 'spider'.

- Glue the buttons on to the spiders to make eyes.

- Make a small hole in the top of each spider's body and attach a long piece of elastic. Hang your spiders from the ceiling and in the windows. Scary!

Pumpkin heads: Jack O' Lanterns or pumpkin heads are important Hallowe'en decorations. 'Jack', according to American legend, was an Irishman who was so mean with his money that he wasn't allowed into heaven. But because he was a known trickster who had played tricks on the Devil himself, he wasn't allowed into hell either! So he was cast out to wander the world for all eternity, neither alive nor dead, with a lantern to light his way.

How to carve a pumpkin:

- Cut a large circle into the top of the pumpkin and carefully remove this lid.

- Scoop out the seeds and the flesh and scrape the inside of the pumpkin until smooth.

- Draw a gruesome face on the outside of the pumpkin using a black marker.

- Carefully cut the face out using a sharp, serrated kitchen knife.

- Cut the top off the pumpkin lid to prevent the candle flame from burning the flesh.

- Place a night-light in the pumpkin, replace the lid and watch the eerie face glow!

Music

Spooky atmospheric tapes are fun to make. Bang boxes shut, rattle heavy (bicycle) chains, scream and make choking noises into a tape recorder. The results will be spectacular.

One year we made a tape which included sounds like coffins closing, chains rattling and banshees wailing (my sister); our seven-year-old neighbour was terrified!

Play spooky stories on tape, such as *Dracula*, *Frankeinstein* or a *Goosebumps* story.

Hallowe'en Games

Apple Bobbing: Fill a bowl half full of water and place on the floor or a table. Each child in turn must grab an apple with his or her teeth and lift it out of the water. The child who grabs the most apples in a given amount of time wins.

Snap Apple: Tie apples in a row on to a broom handle or a piece of wood, which will be held by two adults. Line up the children in a row; they must grab the swinging apple in front of them with their teeth. The first child to grab an apple wins.

Apple Curls Fortune-telling: Peel an apple for each child, keeping the peel all in one piece. Each guest then throws it over their right shoulder; it will form the initial of their future sweetheart!

Gypsy Fortune-telling: An older child or adult dresses up as a fortune-teller, in a cloak with a headscarf and gold hoop earrings. Make a fortune-telling booth by decorating a small room (or a corner of a room) with stars, coloured scarves and blankets. Dim the lighting. In turn each child is told his or her 'fortune' by the 'gypsy'.

Chamber of Horrors: Place special 'horrors' on a chosen table in one of the party rooms. Blindfold the children in turn and invite them to discover the 'horrors' for themselves. Not for the faint hearted!

To create the 'horrors':

- Hang lengths of wool, furry scarves and material from the ceiling – the children must walk through the 'cobwebs'.

- Place plates of cold spaghetti, peeled grapes, cold-water-filled rubber gloves and cotton wool on a table and invite them to touch 'brains', 'eyes', a 'dead man's hand' and 'spider's eggs'!

- Play spooky sound effects in the background.

Hallowe'en Food

Decorate the party table with a black paper table-cloth, decorated with tin-foil stars and orange pumpkin heads cut from orange paper. Decorate paper plates with bats or cats cut from black paper. Make name place cards from small orange pumpkin heads cut from orange card. Hang black paper flying witches and black cats over the table and light the room with candles or night-lights in jam jars. Special Hallowe'en balloons in black and orange can be hung over the table.

Bloody hand sandwiches: You need – loaf of white bread, tomato ketchup, 12 slices of ham.

Place your clean hand on a slice of bread and cut around the impression. Repeat with each slice and butter one side of each 'hand'. Tear a slice of ham to create tattered edges and place on a 'hand'. Add ketchup around the edges to resemble blood and place a 'hand' slice of bread on top.

Monster mush drink: You need – 1 carton of orange juice, 1 carton or 1 jug of blackcurrant juice, 1 bottle Cola, 1 cube of blackcurrant or raspberry jelly

Cut the jelly into small lumps, swirls and worms with a sharp knife. Pour all the juice into a large bowl and add the jelly shapes. Stir well.

Colcannon: A traditional Hallowe'en dish, when coins are wrapped in foil and hidden in the mixture. But watch those teeth! For this recipe, which serves four to six people, you need – 1 white cabbage, 8 potatoes, 4 onions, salt and pepper, 1 pint / 570 ml water, 4 oz (100 g) butter.

Cut the cabbage into four pieces and remove the middle stump. Peel the potatoes and remove the outer layer of the onions. Chop the onions, cabbage and potatoes into slices half an inch thick.

Place a layer of potatoes in the bottom of a large saucepan, add a layer of onions, then a layer or cabbage. Season with a small pinch of salt and pepper. Continue to add layers until all the vegetables are used up. Remember to season each layer.

Pour the water over the vegetables, bring to the boil and simmer for 25-30 minutes, until all the vegetables are tender. Drain the water and mash them together. Place in a serving dish and stir in coins wrapped in tin foil. Drop the butter into the middle and serve piping hot.

Barm brac: At Hallowe'en special items are wrapped and added to the brac to tell your fortune. A wedding-ring means you will be married, a coin wealth, a pea poverty and a thimble that you will never be married!

You need – 4 oz (100 g) soft brown sugar, 8 oz (200 g) mixed fruit, 1 cup tea, 1 egg, 8 oz (200 g) flour (self raising). Preheat the oven to gas mark 4 / 350°F (175°C)

Place the fruit and sugar in a large mixing bowl and soak in the cup of tea for one hour (or longer if possible).

Stir in the egg and the flour gently with a wooden spoon.

Place the mixture in a greased loaf tin and bake for one hour.

Serve warm or cold with butter.

Going-home Presents

At Hallowe'en children traditionally have a 'swag bag' in which they collect all their goodies. Use small paper bags or a circular piece of black paper or material fastened with string. Fill it with sweets, chocolate money and spooky surprises – monster stickers, plastic spiders, trick blood and tiny skeletons.

8 Face Painting

Face painting is a fun activity for any children's party. In the case of younger children an adult can paint their faces. Older children of eight plus may like to paint each other's faces. Basic party faces are not difficult – you don't need to be a great artist – and water-based face paint washes off skin and clothes easily. Face paint, sponges and brushes can be bought in any good art and craft shop – here's what you need:

- Water-based face paints in basic colours – white, black, yellow, red and blue. Metallic gold, silver, colours and glitter are an optional extra.

- A make-up sponge or face painting sponge.

- One fine paintbrush and one thicker one.

- A hair band or scrunchie for longer hair.

To apply a base: Wet the clean sponge and squeeze hard until it is damp but not dripping water. Rub the sponge lightly over the face paint. Dab the paint on to the child's face in gentle strokes. Be careful around the eyes and mouth. Check the face for missed spots and even up the chin line.

To make brush-strokes: Hold the brush like a pencil, close to the bristles. For thin strokes, use the tip of the brush; for thicker lines use the whole flat of the brush.

Easy faces: Study the sketches here and on the foll-owing pages and you will be able to create lions, cats, dogs, princesses, moustashed aliens, bats and Christmas faces. For clowns and teddy bears see page 2.

Lion and Cat

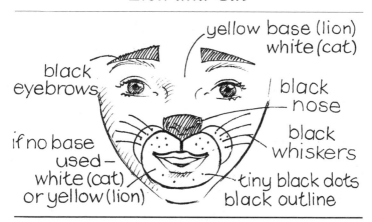

yellow base (lion)
white (cat)

black
eyebrows

black
nose

if no base
used —
white (cat)
or yellow (lion)

black
whiskers

tiny black dots
black outline

Bat

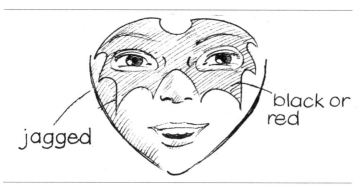

jagged

black or
red

Monster or alien

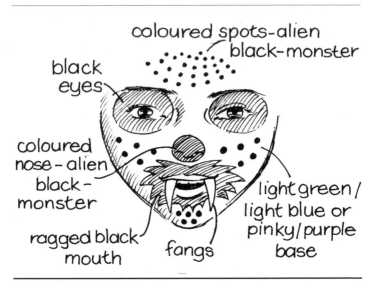

coloured spots-alien
black-monster

black eyes

coloured nose - alien
black - monster

ragged black mouth

fangs

light green / light blue or pinky/purple base

Christmas face

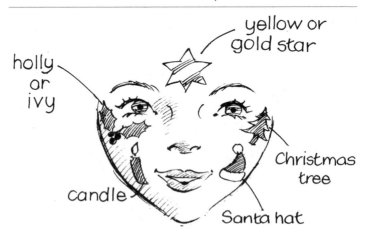

yellow or gold star

holly or ivy

Christmas tree

candle

Santa hat

Dog

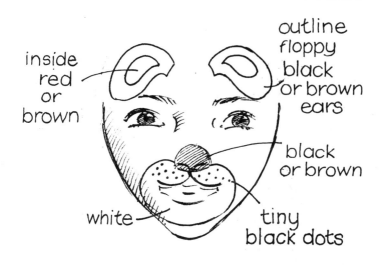

inside red or brown

outline floppy black or brown ears

black or brown

white

tiny black dots

Princess

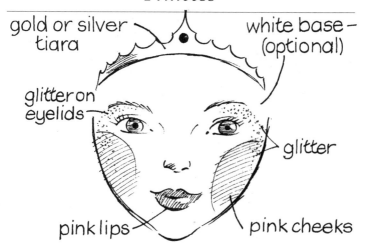

gold or silver tiara

white base – (optional)

glitter on eyelids

glitter

pink lips

pink cheeks

Flower Faces: Try a painting a flower crown on a child's forehead, with these flower shapes.

Daisy: Draw a yellow centre. Then, using the flat of the brush, paint petals, with their points facing towards the central yellow dot.

Rose: Draw a pink or red central swirl, then surround with flat brush-strokes to create petals.

Primrose: Use double yellow brush-strokes to create 'heart' petals around a central dot.

Poppies: Paint a large black central dot. Paint large red petals, in an irregular pattern, around it.

Tulips: Paint tiny red and yellow tulip shapes with triple, flat brush-strokes. Add a thin green stem.

Leaves: Flat brush, strokes in green create leaves. Try small green lines and swirls to create tendrils and vines.

9 Magic Show

Simple magic tricks keep children of five to eight 'spellbound'. Magic shows are easy to perform – all they require are some basic props, a little preparation and a willing 'magician'.

Create a 'magical' atmosphere with a darkened room, lit by night-lights and coloured bulbs. Dress your magician, if he or she is willing, in a black cloak with silver tin-foil stars (a black bin liner can make a great makeshift cloak).

Most toy shops have fun 'magic tricks' for you to buy – you could add these to your own repertoire of the winning tricks which follow.

And now for my first trick ...

The Magic Balloon

Preparation: Blow up a balloon and stick a small piece of sellotape to it.

- Show the audience the 'magic balloon' and tell them that you will prick it with a pin and it won't burst!

- Ask a child to 'test' the pin to see if it is sharp.

- Prick the balloon on the sellotape and it will not pop – *magic!*

(The air will slowly escape from the balloon through the tiny hole. Remember to keep a firm hold on the pin while pricking the balloon.)

The Magic Wall

Rub an inflated balloon on a child's hair. The balloon will now stick to the wall – *magic!*

The balloon can also create some very funny hairstyles – all you need are a few victims. 'Charge' the balloon on the hair and use it to lift and 'style' the locks.

The Magic Banana

Preparation: Take a banana, pierce gently with a toothpick and move it slowly from side to side. This will cut the banana inside without harming the skin. 'Cut ' the banana in several places. Place it in a fruit bowl and note its position.

- Take the magic banana from the fruit bowl and introduce it to the audience, saying, 'Now see before you the magic banana.'

- Wave your hand over it and say the magic word – anything from 'sausages' to 'abracadabra'.

- Ask a child to peel the banana and it will fall into slices in his or her hand – *magic!*

The Magic Dice

A lot of people believe that the number seven has magical powers. And in the case of this trick it's true! On dice, the numbers on the sides directly opposite to each other add up to seven. You can use this fact to amaze and astound young children.

• Throw a dice.

• 'Guess' the number on the opposite (face down) side; eg, for 1 the number is 6, for 2 it's 5.

Now try the trick with more than one dice. The party guests will be amazed at your powers of intuition – *magic!*

The Amazing Prediction

Preparation: You need eleven pieces of paper, an envelope, a pen or pencil and a box – a shoe box is ideal.

• Ask the children for ten famous names. As they call them out disregard what they are saying and write *the same name* (eg, 'Madonna') on each of the ten pieces of paper and fold each over. It is important that the audience do not see what you are writing as they are expecting you to write the names they call out.

• Tell the audience that you will now predict which name will be chosen out of the box. Write the name (the one you have already decided on and have written on all ten sheets of paper) on the extra piece of paper and seal in the envelope.

• Place all the folded sheets in the box. Take out two sheets of paper and pretend to 'read' two of the suggested famous names.

- Ask a member of the audience to pick a piece of paper out of the box and ask him or her to read out the name. (Remember all the names are the same but only you know this.)

- Open your written 'prediction' and show it to the audience – *magic!*

The Magic Cork

Preparation: Take a glass and fill it with water to the very top. It's essential to practise this trick before performing as the first part won't work unless the glass is really brimming over.

- Gently place a cork on the surface of the water. It will stay in the centre.

- Sternly command the cork to move to the edge of the glass.

- Gently pick the cork up, carefully displacing some of the water at the same time.

- Say, 'Mr Cork, will you *please* move to the edge of the glass?'

- Place the cork back in the glass and it *will* move to the edge – *magic!*

The Magic Matchbox

Preparation: Take a matchbox. Slide a match between the cover and the bottom (solid part) of the box, facing the some way as the matches in the box.

- Show the audience all the sides of the closed matchbox.

- Slide the cover off to show the children the matches inside. Hold the extra trapped match with your thumb.

- Slide the cover back on to the matches, keeping the extra match on the outside.

- Ask for a volunteer. Hold the matchbox over his or her hand. Then say the magic word – 'abracadabra'.

- Move your thumb, letting the extra match fall into the child's hand – *magic!*

This trick is a little more difficult, as the extra 'magic' match has to be kept hidden from the view of the audience – it's ideal for those with 'quick' fingers. But try practising on your family until you get it right.

It's magic!

10 Parties outside the Home

You may prefer to hold your party at a children's fun centre or take the boys and girls to the cinema or the zoo. Here are some ideas for parties outside the home.

For details of the venues mentioned and a comprehensive list of others around the country see the appendix.

Ages 3 to 4

Puppet shows: Great entertainment for younger children. The most famous puppet theatre in Ireland is run by the Lambert family in Monkstown, Co Dublin.

Children's play centres: Play centres are good for energetic kids – they include a mixture of slides, bouncing castles, rope bridges and climbing frames. Some centres, such as Bam Bams in Co Dublin, even cater for parties, providing food and drink.

Pet farms: There are pet farms or open farms all over the country. Some allow the children to feed the smaller animals, others have donkey or pony rides. Ideal for younger children, especially those who live in a city or non-farming area.

Ages 5 to 6 plus

Dublin Zoo, wildlife parks and special farms: Dublin Zoo is always popular for parties. Outside Dublin there are wildlife parks and special farms such as the Straffan Butterfly Farm in Co Kildare.

Cinema: A trip to the cinema always rates highly. Choose the film to suit the age-group and the particular children. Most cinemas will offer discounts for parties. For added excitement you could ask the children to come dressed as a character from the film they will be seeing.

Pantomime or show: Children love traditional pantos! Check with the local theatre for details. During the year the arts centre in your area may hold special events – the Ark in Temple Bar in Dublin has wonderful shows for young audiences during the annual Theatre Festival in October. Check with your local arts centre for details.

Museums or historic sites: Some museums are fun for younger children (leave the more 'serious' ones and galleries to the older kids). Try a trip to a local historic site (well-supervised of course!) such as Dalkey Island in south Co Dublin or the Natural History Museum in Dublin; the stuffed animals in this beautifully maintained Victorian setting never cease to amaze young visitors. The Museum of Irish Transport in Killarney, Co Kerry, or Fota Island outside Cork city are also popular choices.

Ages 8 plus

Swimming parties: Take a well-supervised (most important) group of children to the local swimming-pool. Many have discounts for groups or parties.

Activities – bowling alley, ice rink or Quazar laser-gun games: Older party guests enjoy fun, interactive activities. Check for details of party discounts. Some venues also provide party food.

Fire station: A great choice for inquisitive kids and fun for adults too. Apply in writing to your local station. Most will give a tour of the station and its engines to small groups.

Chocolate, glass, or Guinness factory: For something a little different, some manufacturing companies, such as Irish Dresden in Drumcolloher in Co Limerick, will give guided tours of their factories to small groups of children. Check locally for details.

Other ideas for this age-group are:

Castle visits
Day tours on a bus or train
Fishing at a fish farm
Gardens or historic house and grounds
Lighthouse trips (apply in writing)
Pony trekking

See the appendix for other party ideas all over Ireland.

Appendix 1: Trips and Venues

Check opening days, times and cost of your chosen venue well before the party. Ask about group discounts, food and drink. The age group suggested for each place or trip is only a rough guide, so choose carefully to suit your guests' attention-span or needs. Book in advance to avoid disappointment.

Venues are given by county. For other ideas, try local Yellow Pages, *Kids' Day Out* by Bridog Ní Bhuachalla or *The Adventure Guide to Dublin* by Mary Finn.

Co Antrim

Belfast Zoo (3+), Antrim Road, Belfast.
Tel: (08) 01232 776277. *Open all year.*
Causeway Safari Park (5+), Benvarden Road,
Ballymoney. Tel: (08) 01265 41474. *Open Saturdays and Sundays in June; daily July and August.*
Giant's Causeway (8+), Causeway Head, near Bushmills.
Tel: (08) 01265 731855. *Open all year.*
Leslie Hill Heritage Farm and Park (5+), Macfin Road,
Ballymoney. Tel: (08) 012656 66803. *Open Saturdays and Sundays in June; daily July and August.*

Co Armagh

Tannaghmore Gardens and Farms (7+), Silverwood,
Craigavon. Tel: (08) 01762 343244. *Open all year.*

Co Carlow

Ballykealy Open Farm (6+), Ballon. Tel: 0503 59130.
Open by appointment only.
Carrigbeg Riding Stables (8+), Bagenalstown,
Tel: 0503 21962. *Open all year.*

Dunleckney Manor (8+), Bagenalstown. Tel: 0503 21932.
Open July to October.
Graiguecullen Swimming Pool (8+), Graiguecullen.
Tel: 0503 40330 *Open all year.*

Co Cavan

Killykeen Forest Park (7+), Killykeen, Cavan Town.
Tel: 049 32541. *Open all year.*

Co Clare

Aillwee Caves (6+), Ballyvaughan. Tel: 065 77036. *Open
March to November.*
Burren National Park (7+), Kilfenora. Tel: 065 88030.
Open March to October.
Knappogue Castle (7+), Quin. Tel: 061 368103. *Open by
appointment.*

Co Cork

Ballyhoura Mountain Park (6+). Borders of Cork and
Limerick. Tel: 063 91300. *Open all year.*
Bantry House (7+), Bantry Bay. Tel: 027 50047. *Open all
year.*
Charles Fort (8+), Kinsale. Tel: 021 772263. *Open April to
October.*
Fota Wildlife Park (7+), Cobh Road. Tel: 021 812678.
Open April to September; Sundays only October.
Queenstown Project (8+), Cobh. Tel: 021 813612. *Open
by appointment.*
Schull Planetarium (7+), The Community College,
Schull. Tel: 028 28552. *Open by appointment.*
West Cork Model Village and Railway (7+), Inchydoney
Road, Clonakilty. Tel: 023 33224. *Open all year.*

Co Derry

Bananas Play Centre (3+), Pennyburn Industrial Estate,
Derry. Tel: (08) 01504 373731. *Open all year (except
Sundays).*

Foyle Valley Railway Centre (7+), Foyle Road, Derry.
Tel: (08) 01504 265234. *Open May to September on
Tuesdays, Saturdays and Sundays.*

Co Donegal

Bananas Play Centre (3+), Unit 1, Pearse Road,
Letterkenny. Tel: 074 26644. *Open all year.*

Co Down

Ark Open Farm (5+), 296 Bangor Road, Newtownards.
Tel: (08) 01247 820445. *Open all year.*
Butterfly House (7+), Seaforde Nursery, Seaforde.
Tel: (08) 01396 811225. *Open Easter to September.*
Exploris Aquarium (7+), Castle Street, Portaferry.
Tel: (08) 012477 28062. *Open all year.*
Pickie Family Fun Park (5+), The Promenade, Bangor.
Tel: (08) 01247 270069. *Open all year.*

Co Dublin

Ark Children's Cultural Centre (5+), Temple Bar
Dublin 2. Tel: 01 6707788. *All year – check for events.*
Baily Lighthouse (7+), Howth. Tel: 01 8322406. *Open all
year – apply in writing.*
Bam Bams Play Centre (4+), 81 Lower Kilmacud Road.
Tel: 01 2835599. *Open all year.*
Dalkey Island Trips (7+), Coliemore Harbour, Dalkey.
Open summer only – weather permitting.
Dublin Castle (8+), Dame Street, Dublin 2.
Tel: 01 6777129. *Open June to September.*
Dublin Fire Brigade (7+), Tara Street, Dublin 2.
Tel: 01 6778221. *Open all year – apply in writing.*
Dublin Ice Rink (8+), Dolphin's Barn, South Circular
Road, Dublin 8. Tel: 01 4534153. *Open all year.*
**Dublin Writers' Museum and Tara's Palace Dolls'
House** (7+), 18 Parnell Square, Dublin 1.
Tel: 01 8722077. *Open all year.*

Dublin Zoo (4+), Phoenix Park, Dublin 7.
  Tel: 01 6771425. *Open all year.*

Dublinia – The History of Dublin (8+), Christ Church,
  Dublin 8. Tel: 01 6794611. *Open April to September.*

Fort Lucan (2+), Lucan, Outdoor adventure.
  Tel: 01 6280166.

Guinness Hop Store (8+), Crane Street, Dublin 8.
  Tel: 01 4536700. *Open all year.*

Irish Museum of Modern Art (8+), Royal Hospital,
  Kilmainham, Dublin 8. Tel: 01 4536700. *Open all year
  (except Mondays).*

Lambert Puppet Theatre (3+), Clifton Lane,
  Monkstown. Tel: 01 2800974. *Check for details.*

Malahide Castle Fry Model Railway (6+), Malahide.
  Tel: 01 8463779. *Open April to September; weekends and
  Bank Holidays only October to March.*

Marley Park and Model Steam Train (6+), Grange Road,
  Rathfarnham. Tel: 01 942834. *Park open all year; train –
  Saturday during summer.*

Museum of Childhood (7+), 20 Palmerston Park,
  Dublin 6. Tel: 01 4973223. *Open all year.*

National Botanical Gardens (6+), Glasnevin, Dublin 9.
  Tel: 01 8374388. *Open all year.*

National Gallery of Ireland (8+), Merrion Square,
  Dublin 2. Tel: 01 6615133. *Open all year.*

National Museum of Ireland (8+), Kildare Street, Dublin
  2. Tel: 01 6777444. *Open all year (except Mondays).*

National Wax Museum (6+), Granby Row, Parnell
  Square, Dublin 1. Tel: 01 8726340. *Open all year.*

National History Museum (5+), Merrion Row, Dublin 2.
  Tel: 01 6618811. *Open all year (except Mondays).*

Stillorgan Bowl (6+), Stillorgan. Tel: 01 2881656. *Open
  all year.*

Wally Wabbits Play Centre (4+), Pye Centre, Dundrum,
  Dublin 14. Tel: 01 2983470. *Open all year.*

Co Fermanagh

Devenish Island (8+), Enniskillen.
Tel (08) 01232 235000. *Open Easter to September (except Mondays).*
Marble Arch Caves (8+), Enniskillen.
Tel: (08) 01365 348855. *Open March to September.*

Co Galway

Aughnanure Castle (age 8+), Oughterard.
Tel: 091 82214. *Open June to September.*
Connemara National Park (6+), Clifden. Tel: 095 41054.
Open June to August.
Galway Children's Theatre (5+), Seapoint, Salthill.
Tel: 091 524388. *Open during summer.*
Peter Pan Funworld (4+), Wellpark. Tel: 091 756505.
Open all year.

Co Kerry

Crag Cave (7+), Castleisland. Tel: 066 41244. *Open March to October.*
Fenit Seaworld (7+), The Peir, Fenit. Tel: 066 36544. *Open all year.*
Jungle Jim's Adventure World (3+), 20 Pembroke Street, Tralee. Tel: 066 28187. *Open all year.*
Killarney National Park (7+), Killarney. Tel: 064 31440. *Open all year.*
Muckross House (7+), Killarney. Tel: 064 31440. *Open all year.*
Ross Castle (8+), Killarney. Tel: 064 35851. *Open all year.*
Siamsa Tire Theatre (8+), Tralee. Tel: 066 23055. *Check for details of children's programmes.*
Skellig Islands Centre (8+), Valentia Island.
Tel: 066 76306. *Open April to September.*
Tralee and Blennerville Steam Railway (7+), Tralee.
Tel: 066 28888. *Open mid March to October.*
Waterworld (8+), Maharees, Castlegregory. Tel: 066 39292.

Co Kildare

Athy Swimming Pool (8+), Athy. Tel: 0507 31524. *Open all year.*

Castletown House (8+), Celbridge. Tel: 01 6288252. *Open all year.*

Celbridge Abbey Grounds and Model Railway (6+) Celbridge. Tel: 01 6288350. *Open afternoons March to October (except Mondays).*

Greenline Pitch and Putt (8+), Kerdiffstown, Sallins. Tel: 045 879849. *Open all year.*

Japanese Gardens and National Stud (7+), Tully. Tel: 045 521617. *Open Easter to October.*

Morell Farm (6+), Turnings, Straffan. Tel: 01 6288636. *Open all year.*

Redlands Riding Stables (8+), Watergrange. Tel: 045 521570. *Open by appointment.*

Straffan Steam Museum (7+), Lodge Park, Straffan. Tel: 01 6273155. *Open all year.*

Straffan Butterfly Museum (6+), Ovidstown, Straffan. Tel: 01 6271109. *Open May to August and Bank Holidays.*

Co Kilkenny

Dunmore Cave (7+), Ballyfoyle. Tel: 056 67726. *Open March to October.*

Fun Factory (6+), New Street, Kilkenny. Tel: 056 71522.

Jerpoint Abbey (7+), Thomastown. Tel: 056 24623. *Open April to October.*

Kilfane Waterfall (7+), Kilfane, Thomastown. Tel: 056 24558. *Open May to September.*

Kilkenny Castle (7+), Parade, Kilkenny. Tel: 056 21450. *Open April to October.*

Watergate Theatre (6+), Parliament Street, Kilkenny. Tel: 056 61674. *Open all year – check for details.*

Co Laois

Donaghmore Open Farm (5+), Castletown House, Donaghmore. Tel: 0505 46415. *Open by appointment.*
Emo Court and Gardens (7+), Emo.
Tel: 0502 26110. *Open March to October.*
Lutyens Gardens (6+), Ballinakill, Portlaoise.
Tel: 0502 33563. *Open May to September.*

Co Leitrim

Parkes Castle (7+), Dromahair. Tel: 071 64149. *Open March to October.*
Teach Duchais Folk Museum (8+), Drumeela, Carrigallen. Tel: 049 33055. *Open during summer.*

Co Limerick

Celtic Park and Gardens (6+), Foynes Road, Limerick.
Tel: 061 394243. *Open March to November.*
Curraghchase Forest Park (7+), Kilcornan, Pallaskenry.
Tel: 061 396558. *Open all year.*
Glin Castle and Gardens (8+), Glin. Tel: 068 34173.
Open May to June.
Peter Pan Fun World (3+), Cresent Centre, Dooradoyle, Limerick. Tel: 061 301033. *Open all year.*

Co Longford

Longford Sports Complex (8+), Templemichael, Longford. Tel: 043 47000. *Open all year (except Sundays).*
Carriglass Manor (8+), Longford. Tel: 043 45165. *Open by appointment.*

Co Louth

Dundalk Museum (8+), Jocelyn Street, Dundalk.
Tel: 042 27056. *Open all year (except Mondays).*
Millmount Museum (9+), Millmount, Drogheda.
Tel: 041 33097. *Open all year (except Mondays).*

Co Mayo

Bellacorick Bog Train (8+), Bellacorick.
  Tel: 096 53002. *Open May to September.*
Inniskea Island Tours (8+), Bru Chlann Lir, Clogher,
  Belmullet. Tel: 097 85741. *Open during summer.*

Co Meath

Grove Gardens (7+), Fordstown, Kells. Mini Zoo.
  Tel: 046 34276.
Mosney Centre – Go Karts and Amusement Park (7+),
  Mosney. Tel: 841 6666. *Open May to August.*
Newgrange Farm (7+), Slane. Tel: 041 24119. *Open July
  and August; Sundays only May and June.*
Newgrange Passage Grave (8+), Newgrange.
  Tel: 041 24488. *Open March to November.*

Co Monaghan

Castle Leslie (8+), Glaslough. Tel: 047 88109. *Open June
to August.*

Co Offaly

Birr Castle and Gardens (8+), Rosse Row, Birr.
  Tel: 0509 20056. *Open all year.*
Clonmacnoise and West Offaly Railway (7+),
  Blackwater Works, Shannonbridge.
  Tel: 0905 74114. *Open Easter to September.*

Co Roscommon

Open Farm (5+), Tullyboy, Boyle. Tel: 079 68031. *Open
  May to September.*
King House (8+), Boyle. Tel: 079 63242. *Open April to
  October.*

Co Sligo

Lissadell House (8+), Drumcliffe. Tel: 071 63150. *Open
June to September.*

Wild Rose Water Bus Tours (7+), Lough Gill.
Tel: 071 64266. *Open April to October.*

Co Tipperary

Cahir Castle (7+), Cahir. Tel: 052 41011. *Open all year.*
Dundrum Planetarium (7+), Dundrum. Tel: 062 71303.
Open all year.
Mitchelstown Caves (8+), Burncourt, Cahir.
Tel: 052 67246. *Open all year.*
Parson's Green – Pet Field, Playground and Gardens (6+),
Clogheen. Tel: 052 65290. *Open all year.*

Co Tyrone

Altmore Open Farm (7+), 32 Altmore Road, Pomeroy.
Tel (08) 01868 758977. *Open all year.*
Ulster History Park (6+), Omagh. Tel (08) 01662 668188.
Open all year.

Co Waterford

Funderworld (3+), Cork Road, Waterford. Tel: 051 71117.
Open all year.
Laserworld (8+), Tramore. Tel: 051 386565. *Open all year.*

Co Westmeath

Athlone Castle and Museum (7+), Athlone,
Tel: 0902 92912. *Open May to September.*
Ben Breeze Open Farm (6+), Fore. Tel: 044 66338. *Open
by appointment.*
Glendeer Open Farm (6+), Drum, Athlone.
Tel: 0902 37147. *Open April to September.*

Co Wexford

Ballyhack Castle (8+), Ballyhack, Arthurstown.
Tel: 051 389468. *Open April to September.*
Ballylane Farm and Picnic Barn (8+), New Ross.
Tel: 051 21315. *Open May to August.*

Dunbrody Famine Ship (8+), New Ross. Tel: 051 425239.
Guillemot Lightship Maritime Museum (6+), Kilmore
Quay, Wexford. Tel: 053 29655. *Open June to September.*
Johnstown Castle Gardens (6+), Pierstown.
Tel: 053 42888. *Open all year.*
Kia Ora Mini Farm (5+), Gorey. Tel: 055 21166.
Yola Farm and Playground (5+), Tagoat. Tel: 053 31177.
Open May to September.

Co Wicklow

Annamoe Park and Play Area (6+), Roundwood.
Tel: 0404 45145. *Open June to August; weekends only May
and September.*
Ballinagee Open Farm (6+), Waterfall Road, Enniskerry.
Tel: 01 2869154. *Open Easter to October.*
Ballygannon ('Glenroe') Open Farm (4+), Kilcoole. Tel:
01 2872288. *Open all year; weekends only in winter.*
An Boithrin Cam Open Farm (6+), Valleymount,
Blessington. Tel: 045 67332. *Open by appointment.*
Clara Lara Funpark (5+), Clara Vale, Rathdrum.
Tel: 0404 46161. *Open April to September.*
Powerstown Gardens and Adventure Playground (5+),
Enniskerry. Tel: 01 2867676. *Open March to October.
Waterfall and picnic area open all year.*

Appendix 2: Party Services

Cakes and catering, balloons and bouncing castles, enter-tainers, face-painters, and party planners – here's a handy round-up of services available around the country, listed by phone area. But as it is only a small selection of what's on offer, check your local Yellow Pages for further details.

01 Area – Dublin

Cakes and Catering
Aylesbury Home Bakery, D 24. Tel: 01 4598572.
Boston Bakery, 36 Drumcondra Road Lower, D 9.
   Tel: 01 8305828.
Cake Craft, 4 Ulverton Close, Dalkey. Tel: 01 2841137.
Cakes and Co, 25 Rock Hill, Blackrock. Tel: 01 2836544.
Celebration Cakes, 45 Sundrive Road, Kimmage, D12.
   Tel: 01 4921216.
Country Bake, 35 Castle Street, Dalkey, Co Dublin.
   Tel: 01 2852009.
Dial-A-Cake, 6 Ridge Road, Ballybrack, Co Dublin.
   Tel: 01 2820404.

Balloons and Party Shops
The Balloon Man, 61d Heather Road, Sandyford
   Industrial Estate, D 18. Tel: 01 2957522.
Barry's Balloon and Party Shop, 16 Prospect Road,
   Glasnevin, D 9. Tel: 01 8301700.
Party Shop, beside Kiely's Pub, Donnybrook, D 4.
   Tel: 01 2693500.
Phyllis's Balloons, 355 Ballyfermot Road, D 10.
   Tel: 01 6264945.

Bouncing Castles and Entertainment

Abbey Bouncing Castles, D3. Tel: 01 8323924 /
   088 612026.

Bumble's Castles, Killiney. Tel: 01 2350394.

Laser Karaoke, 106 Seskin View Road, Tallagh, D 24.
   Tel: 01 4513274.

Entertainers

A for Magic, 73 Deanswift Road, Glasnevin, D 11.
   Tel: 01 8379643.

ABC Magic, 33 Corrig Avenue, Dun Laoghaire.
   Tel: 01 2845300.

Anna Bananas Clown and Face Painter, Dun Laoghaire.
   Tel: 01 2845357.

Eugene Corr Magic Show, 50 Brian Road, Marino,
   Dublin 3. Tel: 01 8338732.

Dave Young Magician, Walkinstown Parade, Dublin 2.
   Tel: 01 4508210.

Giggles 'n Grins. Tel: 01 8425121 / 087 479684.

Julie Rose McCormick, Puppeteer, Wayside, Kilcoole,
   Co Wicklow. Tel: 01 2804347.

The Magic Man, Killiney. Tel: 2858182.

Quentin Reynolds Magic and Punch and Judy,
   11 Orchard Terrace, D 7. Tel: 01 8680058.

Tiggy's Parties – Face Painting, Balloon Sculpture–Tarva,
   Green Road, Dalkey. Tel: 01 2851514.

Party Planners

The Bar Man Party Planners, Dublin. Tel: 1890 227626 /
   087 530902.

Dial-a-Party, 10 Woodford, Brewery Road, Blackrock,
   Tel: 087 531566.

Funarama Event Theme Packs, 61d Heather Road,
   Sandyford IE , Dublin 18. Tel: 01 2957342.

02 Area

Cakes and Catering
Celebration Cakes, 3 Winthrop Arcade, Cork.
  Tel: 021 270991.
Fordes Confectionery, 39 Riverview Estate, Ballyvolane,
  Cork. Tel: 021 501983.
Hassett's Bakery, Ballycureen I E, Kinsale Road, Cork.
  Tel: 021 317017.
The Patisserie, Main Street, Carrigaline, Co Cork.
  Tel: 021 372306.

Balloons
Balloon Surprise, 2 Washington Street, Cork.
  Tel: 021 275330.

Entertainment
Brendan Manning Entertainments, 42a Patrick Street,
  Cork. Tel: 021 276465.

04 Area

Cakes and Catering
Pat the Baker, Granard, Co Longford. Tel: 043 86523.
Sweet Sensations, Blackhouse Centre, Clanbrassil Street,
  Dundalk, Co Louth. Tel: 042 33510.

05 Area

Cakes and Catering
Barron's Bakery, The Square, Cappoquin, Co Waterford.
  Tel: 058 54045.
Jean's Cakes, Kellyville Shopping Centre, Portlaoise.
  Tel: 0502 21299.
The Pantry, Kieran Street, Kilkenny. Tel: 056 62250.

Entertainers
Moon and Sixpence Puppet Theatre, Killinan House,
  Thurles, Co Tipperary. Tel: 0504 22056.

06 Area

Cakes and Catering

Breen Cakes and Catering, 10a Flemings Lane, Killarney,
   Co Kerry. Tel: 064 33881
Kakes and Kandies, Grenville, Clontarf Place, Limerick.
   Tel: 061 310016.

Entertainers

Dandelion Puppets, Ballyblood, Tulla, Co Clare.
   Tel: 065 25566.

07 Area

Cakes and Catering

Gavin's Cakes, Bridge Street, Westport, Co Mayo.
   Tel: 098 26114.
Queen of Cakes, The Port Road, Letterkenny.
   Tel: 074 24418.

Balloons

Party Creations, 34 Woodfield, Barna, Co Galway.
   Tel: 091 591007 / 0872224813.

Entertainers

Padmini Magic, 6 Quay Street, Galway. Tel: 091 65698.

**Whether you're ordering cakes or magicians,
BE SPECIFIC.
And put your order in writing.**

Index

Author

SARAH WEBB is the Children's Marketing Manager of Eason. She lives in Dalkey, eight miles south of Dublin city, in a converted coach house, with her son Sam. Sarah is a founding member of Children's Books Ireland and organises children's book events for adults and children.

In her spare time she likes reading, cooking (and eating) and sailing.

Sarah's first book was *Kids Can Cook*, a great success with children of all ages (adults too!). She is now working on a follow up – *Kids Can Cook Around the World*.